# METHODS OF EARLY GOLF ARCHITECTURE

The Selected Writings of Alister MacKenzie,
H.S. Colt, and A.W. Tillinghast

Presented by **Coventry House Publishing**

ISBN: 0615829295
ISBN-13: 978-0615829296

# CONTENTS

# CHAPTER 1

## Characteristics of a Golf Architect

*"He should, above all, have a sense of proportion and be able to come to a prompt decision as to what is the greatest good to the greatest number." – Alister MacKenzie*

*By Alister MacKenzie:*

There are many and varied qualities required for the making of a successful golf architect.

In the first place, he must have an intimate knowledge of the theory of playing the game. He need not be himself a good player. He may have some physical disability which prevents him becoming so, but as the training of the golf architect is purely mental and not physical, this should not prevent him from being a successful golf course architect. In any case, the possession of a vivid imagination, which is an absolute essential in obtaining success, may prevent him attaining a position among the higher ranks of players. Everyone knows how fatal imagination is in playing the game. Let the fear of socketing once enter your head, and you promptly socket every shot afterwards.

His knowledge of the game should be so intimate that he knows instinctively what is likely to produce good golf and good golfers. He must have more than a passing acquaintance with the best courses and the best golfing holes. It is not only necessary that he should play them, but study them and analyze the features which make them what they are. He must have a sense of proportion and be able to differentiate between essentials and non-essentials. He should be able to distinguish between those features which are of supreme importance in the making of a hole and those which are of less value.

He must have judgment in the choice of features which can be readily and cheaply reproduced, and not those which are impossible to construct without an inordinate expenditure of labor.

How frequently has one seen hundreds of pounds wasted in a futile attempt to reproduce the Alps, the Himalayas, or the Cardinal! Features of this kind look absolutely out of place unless the surrounding ranges of hills which harmonize with them are also reproduced. To do this would involve the expenditure of hundreds of thousands of pounds. How often are attempts made to copy a hole and the subtle slopes and undulations which are the making of the original overlooked!

The golf course architect must have the sporting instinct, and if he has had a training in many and varied branches of sport, and has analyzed those characteristics which provide a maximum of pleasurable excitement in them, so much the better. It is essential that he should eliminate his own game entirely, and look upon all constructional work in a purely impersonal manner.

He should be able to put himself in the position of the best player that ever lived, and at the same time be extremely sympathetic towards the beginner and long-handicap player.

He should, above all, have a sense of proportion and be able to come to a prompt decision as to what is the greatest good to the greatest number.

He should not be unduly influenced by hostile criticism, but should give the most sympathetic consideration to criticism of a constructive nature. Not infrequently a long-handicap man makes a brilliant suggestion which can often be utilized in a modified form.

A knowledge of psychology gained in the writer's medical training has been of great service in estimating what is likely to give the greatest pleasure to the greatest number.

It by no means follows that what appears to be attractive at first sight will be permanently so. A good golf course grows on one like good painting, good music, etc.

The ideal golf architect should have made a study, from a golfing point of view, of agricultural chemistry, botany, and geology. He should also have some knowledge of surveying, map reading, and the interpretation of aerial photographs.

———◆◆———

The expert in golf architecture has to be intimately conversant with the theory of playing the game, but this has no connection with the physical skill in playing it. An ideal golf expert should not only have a knowledge of botany, geology, and particularly agricultural chemistry, but should also have what might be termed an artistic temperament and vivid imagination. We all know that there is nothing so fatal in playing golf as to have a vivid imagination, but this and a sufficient knowledge of psychology to enable one to determine what is likely to give the greatest pleasure to the greatest number are eminently desirable in a golf architect. The training of the expert should be mental, not physical.

---

Golf architecture is a new art closely allied to that of the artist or the sculptor, but also necessitating a scientific knowledge of many other subjects.

In the old days, many golf courses were designed by prominent players, who after a preliminary inspection of the course simply placed pegs to represent the position of the sites for the suggested tees, greens, bunkers, etc. The whole thing was completed in a few hours, and the best results could hardly have been expected, and in fact never were obtained by these methods.

The modern designer, on the other hand, is likely to achieve the most perfect results and make the fullest use of all the natural features by more up-to-date methods.

After a preliminary inspection or inspections in the calm and quiet of his own study with an ordnance map and, if possible, aeroplane photographs in front of him, he visualizes every feature. He is then not so likely to be obsessed by details, but gives everything its due proportionate value. He then evolves his scheme and pays a second visit to the ground, and, if necessary, modifies his ideas according to the appearance on the spot.

---

A little knowledge is especially dangerous thing in links' architecture. One of our greatest troubles in dealing with the committees of the old-established seaside courses is that their world-renowned reputation (not due to any virtue of their own, but entirely owing to the natural advantages of their links) makes them think themselves competent judges of a golf course.

They ask for a report and plan of suggested improvements, and then imagine they have grasped the ideas of the designer, and proceed to make a horrible hash of it. I do not know a single seaside course which has been remodeled in anything like the way it should have been remodeled.

The best artificially constructed seaside course I know is the Eden (Mr. Colt's) Course at St. Andrews. There are few of the crowds of players who, notwithstanding its youth, already congregate on it realize how much is due to artificiality and how little to nature. All the best ground at St. Andrews had been previously seized for the three older courses—the Old, the New, and the Jubilee—and yet it compares favorably with any of them. This is entirely due to the fact that not only was it designed by Mr. Colt, but the construction work was done by men who had been trained under him and worked under his supervision.

It is much better that construction work should be done by men without any knowledge of the subject than by those partly trained.

There is a yarn told about two rival constructors of golf courses: One of them was admiring the other's greens, and remarked that "he never managed to get his green-keeper to make the undulations as natural looking." The other replied that "it was perfectly easy; he simply employed the biggest fool in the village and told him to make them flat."

I believe the real reason St. Andrews Old Course is infinitely superior to anything else is owing to the fact that it was constructed when no one knew anything about the subject at all, and since then it has been considered to sacred to be touched. What a pity it is that the natural advantages of many seaside courses have been neutralized by bad designing and construction work!

# CHAPTER 2

## Psychology of Design

*"The designer of a course should start off on his work in a sympathetic frame of mind for the weak, and at the same time be as severe as he likes with the first-class player." – H.S. Colt*

*By H.S. Colt:*

This is a somewhat dangerous subject to attempt to write about, owing to the innumerable opinions held by golfers of every degree concerning the individual merits of various courses. However, the golf course architect soon realizes how impossible it is to please everyone, and sifts quickly the chaff from the wheat in the matter of suggestions appertaining to his work.

---

In this connection it may be well to bear in mind that golf is primarily a pastime and not a penance, and that the player should have a chance of extracting from a game the maximum amount of pleasure with the minimum amount of discomfort as punishment for his evil ways. He will not obtain this pleasure unless you provide plenty of difficulties; but surely there is no need for vindictiveness. And just think how pleasant it is to hop over a bunker at times, and occasionally hit a wild shot and have a chance of recovery! There is opportunity for much needed mercy even to erratic golfers.

———————•———————

Some few years ago it was a very common idea that the first-class player was the only person to be considered when the course was laid out. Considering how few they are in number, it often strikes one how extraordinarily successful they were in getting their way. But recently the vast number of those in receipt of odds have become more alive to the possession of their power. They have even become infected by the present unrest in the labor market, and during a recent railway strike the members of a club were known to rise in a body and insist upon the restitution of a certain hole, which they considered had been unjustly taken away from them. Courses have no doubt been getting more and more difficult for the average player. His golf has in some cases been a dismal progress from the rough to a bunker, and from a bunker to the rough, hole after hole. He has very likely chosen a pleasant spring day for a little relaxation and pleasure, and returns to his home at night in a jaded and almost hopeless frame of mind. It is by no means impossible to give a weak player every opportunity of enjoying the game within his powers, and at the same time to provide a test of golf for Harry Vardon or James Braid at his very best. To do this, the designer of a course should start off on his work in a sympathetic frame of mind for the weak, and at the same time be as severe as he likes with the first-class player. The more frequently he stamps on the mediocre shot of the latter, so much the better, provided that he does not become vindictive.

I will attempt to show how this can be done. Let us start with the tee shots. It is certainly amusing to have a fair number of carries from the teeing grounds; but if these are to be of any use as a test of length to the first-class driver, they are certain to be impossible to the short player. Therefore if we want to have a carry of say, 165 yards or more, let us provide a path of safety, whilst giving advantage in the subsequent play of the hole to the player who accomplishes the test provided. The 3rd hole at Sunningdale is an example of this.

Then, let us take the case of lateral hazards. These can be made at such a distance from the tee that the weak player very seldom reaches them.

Or take the instance of a central hazard with a path on either side. This class of bunker is always open to criticism from the man who hits a long, straight shot down the center of the course, without having sufficient intelligence in his head to know that the proper line is to the left or to the right, as the case may be, and that if he takes the wrong line, he deserves no sympathy. Well, in the case of such a hazard the weak player can be kept out of it by placing it beyond the limits of his drive; in fact, in designing the bunkering of a course the object should be to catch the bad or mediocre shot of the good player and punish the long-handicap man for bad strokes less than the former. Give the short player as much pleasure as you can by providing short carries off the tee (almost negligible quantities for the good player); he always appreciates them, and he is sure to find quite enough difficulty in the remainder of the course on his own account. The giver of odds has, as a rule, a big advantage when playing a match on the handicap points, and we do not want to accentuate this by giving the receiver of odds too much to do on his way round the course.

## By Alister MacKenzie:

I notice a well-known club, in forming a golf course, state that the committee have decided to lay it out themselves, as they are afraid of a golf architect making it too difficult for the average player. Now this is precisely what the modern golf architect does not do; he in particular adopts a most sympathetic attitude to the beginner and long-handicap player, but at the same time attempts to make the course interesting to all sorts and conditions of players. It is characteristic of the modern architect that he always leaves a broad and pleasurable road that leads to destruction—that is, sixes and sevens on the card of the long-handicap player—but a straight and narrow path which leads to salvation—that is, threes and fours for the plus man.

———•———

One can readily imagine what would be the ultimate result of a course laid out by an average committee composed of scratch, three, four, and eight handicap men. They are, most of them (probably subconsciously), prejudiced against any hazard being constructed which they are likely to get into themselves, but they are all unanimous in thinking that the poor devil with a twenty-four handicap should be left out of consideration altogether. The final result is neither fish, flesh, fowl, nor even good red herring.

*By A. W. Tillinghast:*

It is not necessary to attempt a description of those early American courses, with featureless greens, mathematically correct and symmetrical bunkers and the ridiculous little bandbox teeing grounds. They are of the past, but they served their purpose. The golf courses which we Americans are constructing today are very different, and so carefully are they built, after a thoughtful preparation of plans, that some of our productions are not surpassed even in the old home of golf.

For a long time the greatest obstacle in the way of modern courses in America was the opposition of the mediocre player. He fancied that any attempt to stiffen the courses must make them so difficult that the play would be beyond his powers. But now he realizes that the modern golf architect is keeping him and his limitations in mind all the while he is cunningly planning problems which require the expert to display his greatest skill in negotiating holes in par figures. We are planning and building not to penalize very poor strokes, but rather those which are nearly good. If our holes are of proper distances as dictated by natural conditions the duffer who misses a stroke cannot be figured as a serious factor, so why add to his discomfiture?

"But how may this be accomplished?" is a most natural question for you to ask. Let me attempt a simple and brief explanation, for in the limited space of these tabloid articles, elaborate analysis is impossible. Instead of relying on hazards which extend directly across the line of play we are building them diagonally. It is obvious that these diagonal hazard lines present a much longer carry at one end that at the other, and all carries between the two points vary. In the placement of the short carry we consider the light hitter, and as he stands prepared to play at such a hazard, he is to be the judge of the distance which he may successfully attempt. After a while, as he finds his game improving, it is natural that he becomes more ambitious, and he attempts greater things which he knows will be adequately rewarded, for the hazards guarding the approaches to the green are placed in such a manner as to grade the benefits of length and accuracy. In brief, every player gets exactly what may be coming to him and is not necessary for anyone to bite off more than he can swallow.

The old-fashioned cross bunker always leers at the player with a "You must." The modern diagonal hazard shows even a more ferocious face at one end as it says to the scratch man, "You should." But all along to the short end it is saying, "You may."

# CHAPTER 3

## Deciding Where to Build

*"The cry of, 'It just can't be done here!' has hindered the proper development of courses to a lamentable extent in many sections." – A.W. Tillinghast*

*By A.W. Tillinghast:*

In the early days of golf construction, the usual procedure was to confine the work to the meadowlands and open, but nowadays whole forests and jungles are cut through by fairways. Particularly is this true in the South, and I have recollections of Davista where I was turned loose in a mass of tropical vegetation which was so dense as to seem almost impenetrable. The last of the clearing was accomplished in the winter of 1915, and they were playing golf there a year later.

———

When the golfer of today rolls up to his country club in a fine motor car, it is improbable that he give a single thought to the condition of that same road before the course was built. It must be remembered that usually the courses are located back from public roads, often miles away from main thoroughfares. In 1923, in the province of

Quebec in the Laurentians, it was necessary for me to take a twenty-mile road twice a day over a road which was absolutely cruel. It was early in the winter, but before the snows, and consequently all the summer camps were closed. None but the native habitants was met with. On my first day there I noticed the apparent anxiety of the driver of our Ford to make an early start for the village. He drove like a mad man, and it would be difficult to imagine a rougher voyage. As it was, we passed absolutely no one on the road going in the opposite direction, and it is safe that none passed us going our way. But the seeming desolation of the country surprised me, although occasionally a head would appear at a window. Afterwards I found out that this was the one day in the year when, according to the habitant belief, the dead left their graves and, burrowing like moles, did something or other subterraneanly; possibly visited each other. But that driver was taking no chances, particularly after dusk. Yet in a year or two that same awful road became as fine as any state highway, and led to a country club.

Sometimes in getting back to a prospective site for a golf course the way is little more than a trail through the woods, where even a Ford cannot go, and then it is a case of riding shank's mare. In 1923 at Lakewood, near Cleveland, Ohio, there was a dirt road, which ran for probably a half-mile back from the main thoroughfare. After a storm it was absolutely impassable for any sort of car. A year later in December, I rode over this same road, paved entirely for a distance of two miles, I should say, until it connected two roads. There was no reason in the world for paving but for the fact that a new country club opened there during that past summer.

In 1907, a sleigh took me over a distance of twenty miles, and it is my candid belief that we did not pass a score of houses after the first five miles. With the mercury showing eighteen below zero and a rough road it was tough sledding. Today that entire country has been opened up because a golf course was built back there in the woods. You could not wish for a better road, and houses? Plenty! These references to roads in these recollections are intended only to indicate the great power which a golf course displays in opening up almost unheard of corners of the land.

*By H.S. Colt:*

Nothing appeals to the enthusiast so much as to be taken to a large area of suitable land with the idea of making a course there; but he does not have too many chances of creating something really good, as the majority of sites are rather depressing. If the land is suitable, there is not enough of it; or if the materials be ample, they are moderate in quality. The quantity of land required depends very largely upon its shape, as if square it will be difficult to use it up satisfactorily, but a strip two hundred yards in width is easier to deal with, especially if somewhat circular.

# CHAPTER 4

## The Design Process

*"The course should be so interesting that even the plus man is constantly stimulated to improve his game in attempting shots he has hitherto been unable to play." – Alister MacKenzie*

*By H.S. Colt:*

My own method is first to view the land and walk over it once or twice, and inspect it very carefully, but not to lay out a single hole; then to make a second visit, having considered the scheme in the meantime, and on that occasion to settle, if possible, the framework, and take two or three days to do so, leaving the bunkering in great part for a subsequent visit. Critics may think this too elaborate and expensive; but let them remember the thousands of pounds wasted in the past, and the cost of two or three extra days is not worth consideration, especially if it is a big scheme and several thousands of pounds are to be expended upon it. Even if only a few hundreds are to be spent, it is worth while doing the work properly, and it is impossible to do this unless a considerable amount of time is given to it.

The first thing to do is to settle upon the site for the clubhouse, and this occasionally presents great difficulty. I always favor a fine view from the club windows, and have more than once done battle over this with those favoring only the utilitarian side—such points as nearness to a railway station or very easy access; but these matters have, of course, to be considered carefully, and it is no good perching a clubhouse on a crow's nest.

If the clubhouse site is settled, it is obviously an easy matter to select the first tee; and if the tenth tee is anywhere near, it is of advantage, especially for a club to be used by business men, as there will be two starting points, and in clubs of this description, where a large number arrive about the same time, this is an important matter.

Personally, I like a fairly long, plain-sailing hole for the first one, and think that a short hole is out of place, as if it is a good one it ought to be difficult, and it seems unfair to ask much of a man who has just stepped out of a train or motor car. A couple of long holes at the commencement get the players away from the first tee, and this is desirable from a secretary's point of view, as if his members cannot start, they always become critical and impatient. After that the sequence of the holes does not matter, and what we have to look for are four or five good short holes, several good length two-shot holes, varying from an extra-long brassie shot for the second to a firm half-iron shot, one or two three-shot holes, and two or three difficult drive-and-pitch holes. A fairly equal distribution between what I have designated as good length two-shot holes and the others of all degrees seems to me about right. What we want to have is variety, gained by utilizing all the best natural features of the land, and alternating the holes of various lengths. If possible, the short

holes can be divided between the odd and the even num-
bers, so as to give the partners in a foursome a share of
each. It is, moreover, advisable to play a long three-shot
hole down the prevailing wind rather than against it. And
let us endeavour to avoid the zigzag backwards and forwards, and also holes of a similar character to each other,
so that if a stranger come to our course he may go away
remembering each hole by a distinctive feature. Some
courses I can never remember—you just hit the ball many
times out in the same direction over similar ground, and
then hit it back again; whereas on other courses there is no
difficulty in remembering the various holes because of the
distinctive features. I personally dislike blind shots on a
course. However, it may be quite impossible to avoid one
or two, but it is not necessary to select them for short
holes. To hit the ball over a mountain, and then see an
opponent, who is younger in years and more active in
limb, climb quickly to the crest and watch one's ball gather
pace and reach an unknown bunker on the blind side of
the obstacle, is enough to make even the imperturbable
James Braid annoyed; but, no doubt, this sort of thing
does not occur to him. It would give me but little pleasure
to watch Harry Vardon at his best if I could not see what
was happening to the ball when it reached the ground. A
really skilful player can so wonderfully control the move-
ments of the ball after it reaches the ground. It is always
entertaining to watch a great player's methods when he is
approaching the hole, and quite impossible to get the
same amount of pleasure when thirty feet of sand blocks
the view. Golf consisting of a blind "smack" over one
mountain, followed by a blind "punch" over another, gives
me about as much pleasure to watch as a game of ping-
pong. Good play and bad play are, moreover, equalized to

some extent, as there can never be quite the same chance for the good player to show his extra skill under such conditions. But here, again, for the sake of variety, a blind tee shot may be beneficial once or twice in the round. I would always sacrifice much on this account, but not to the extent of a blind short hole. If variety be strongly developed, we also promote the best feature of the game—different classes of strokes under varying conditions. This is the real reason why golf has become so popular not only at home, but all over the world, and it is on account of this that people do not become bored with the game. So the designer of a course has one clear duty; to try to create fresh holes of interest, and not reproduce, with unsuitable materials, holes similar to those already in existence. Some think, no doubt, that he is quite an unnecessary, and very likely a vexatious, appendage to the game. I was rather amused to read lately, in a very popular morning paper, an article in which mention was made of a course on the west coast. The writer, after being good enough to describe its merits, ended up his article devoutly thankful that no golf course architect had been allowed to meddle with it. The reader can guess at the source of my amusement.

---

There is, however, one great feature that appeals to me—the elasticity of a course; and in designing the framework it is better to walk forward to the next teeing ground, and not to retrace one's steps after playing a hole. This, no doubt, is not by any means always advisable, as a good natural feature may be lost for the next tee shot; but it gives a better chance of making "back" teeing grounds to be used under special conditions. There is no doubt that a series of tees, whereby the length of a hole can be altered with varying conditions, is an advantage. If we take a new course, for instance, the run of the ball will increase with the age of the links, as the surface of the ground becomes firmer with play. The distance of a tee shot will also vary enormously in summer and winter. There were several cases of drives of about 350 yards during the summer of 1911 with the new heavy rubber-cored balls, which in summer now alter so largely the length of a course, so far as the player is concerned. Two or three years ago it was thought that a hole of about 400 yards was one which required two full shots to reach the green. The 18th hole at Sunningdale is now of nearly that length, and during the drought of the year just mentioned Jack White drove this hole from the tee on more than one occasion. So that at the holes where, under normal conditions, there is no long carry off the tee it will be advantageous to be able to obtain more length by using a back tee to suit the varying conditions of the surface of the ground, and also possibly the wind. It will be easier to do this if, after playing a hole, we usually walk forward to the next tee; but at the holes where there is already a long carry from the ordinary tee it is obviously impossible to arrange for much extra length, and when cross hazards are made for compulsory carries in playing the second shots these are the occasions for their use. The length of the drive is no doubt sacrificed, as under abnormal conditions a long hitter will be able to reach the subsequent cross hazard. He must play short, and if he is so foolish as not to do so, he probably gains intense satisfaction by telling as many of his fellow members as will listen to him the details of his great feat; while if he is not a member of the green committee, that body is no doubt referred to in uncomplimentary terms. He is satisfied, and the man who plays with judgment is also satisfied, as he has a more amusing second shot to play by reason of his self-denial on the tee. If, however, there were many examples of this class of hole on the links, long driving would be at a discount; but two or three holes of this description add to the interest of the game, and we cannot afford to sacrifice everything to the length of the tee shot. The new ball, and very likely a little more experience, have made me modify my opinions about the compulsory carry for the second shot, of which, within proper limits, the Editor of *Golf Illustrated* has always been a strong supporter.

———•◦•———

It is impossible to give any definite rules on laying out a course, or to state what length it should be, as everything must depend upon the nature of the materials in each individual case. Anything round about six thousand yards seems to be long enough, even with the new-fashioned ball. It is obvious that there are many bad long courses and many very good short courses, and length has very little to do with merit.

## By Alister MacKenzie:

As the truest economy consists in finality, it is interesting to consider the essential features of an ideal golf course. Some of them are suggested now:
1. The course, where possible, should be arranged in two loops of nine holes.
2. There should be a large proportion of good two-shot holes, two or three drive-and-pitch holes, and at least four one-shot holes.
3. There should be little walking between the greens and tees, and the course should be arranged so that in the

first instance there is always a slight walk forwards from the green to the next tee; then the holes are sufficiently elastic to be lengthened in the future if necessary.

4. The greens and fairways should be sufficiently undulating, but there should be no hill climbing.
5. Every hole should have a different character.
6. There should be a minimum of blindness for the approach shots.
7. The course should have beautiful surroundings, and all the artificial features should have so natural an appearance that a stranger is unable to distinguish them from nature itself.
8. There should be a sufficient number of heroic carries from the tee, but the course should be arranged so that the weaker player, with the loss of a stroke or portion of a stroke, shall always have an alternative route open to him.
9. There should be infinite variety in the strokes required to play the various holes—viz., interesting brassie shots, iron shots, pitch and run-up shots.
10. There should be a complete absence of the annoyance and irritation caused by the necessity of searching for lost balls.
11. The course should be so interesting that even the plus man is constantly stimulated to improve his game in attempting shots he has hitherto been unable to play.
12. The course should be so arranged that the long-handicap player, or even the absolute beginner, should be able to enjoy his round in spite of the fact that he is piling up a big score.
13. The course should be equally good during winter and summer, the texture of the greens and fairways should

be perfect, and the approaches should have the same consistency as the greens.

———————•·•———————

It is not as common an error to make blind holes as formerly. A blind tee shot may be forgiven, or a full shot to the green on a seaside course, when the greens can be located by the position of the surrounding hummocks, but an approach shot should never be blind, as this prevents an expert player, except by a fluke, from placing his approach so near the hole that he gets down in one putt.

Blind holes on an inland course, where there are no surrounding sand hills to locate the green, should never be permitted, but an even more annoying form of blindness is that which is so frequent on inland courses—that is, when the flag is visible but the surface of the green cannot be seen. On a green of this description, no one can possibly tell whether the flag is at the back, middle, or front of the green, and it is particularly aggravating to play your shot expecting to find it dead, and to discover that your ball is at least twenty yards short.

On a seaside course there may be a certain amount of pleasurable excitement in running up to the top of a hillock in the hope of seeing your ball near the flag, but this is a kind of thing one gets rather tired of as one grows older.

*By A. W. Tillinghast:*

In laying out a course which is to be turfed with Bermuda, the architect has to remember that his distances may not be so great as those on northern links, for a ball gets but little run, and a course of six thousand yards in those parts would demand as much vigorous play as one three or four hundred yards longer over northern turf.

# CHAPTER 5

---

# Utilizing Natural Features

*"The finest courses in existence are natural ones."*
*– Alister MacKenzie*

*By Alister MacKenzie:*

The great thing in constructing golf courses is to ensure variety and make everything look natural. The greatest compliment that can be paid to a greenkeeper is for players to think his artificial work is natural. On Alwoodley and Moortown, practically every green and every hummock has been artificially made, and yet it is difficult to convince the stranger that this is so. I remember a chairman of the green committee of one of the best-known clubs in the North telling me that it would be impossible to make their course anything like Alwoodley, as there we had such a wealth of natural hillocks, hollows, and undulations. It was only with great difficulty that I was able to persuade him that, to use an Irishism, these natural features which he so much admired had all been artificially created. I have even heard one of the members of our own green committee telling a well-known writer on golf that the hummocks surrounding one of our greens had always been there: He himself had forgotten that he had been present when the site for them had been pegged out.

———•———

One of the best-known writers on golf has recently been jeering at golf architects for attempting to make beautiful bunkers. If he prefers ugly bunkers, ugly greens, and ugly surroundings generally he is welcome to them, but I don't think for an instant that he believes what he is writing about, for at the same time he talks about the beauties of natural courses. The chief object of every golf architect or greenkeeper worth his salt is to imitate the beauties of nature so closely as to make his work indistinguishable from nature itself.

———•———

The finest courses in existence are natural ones. Such courses as St. Andrews, and the championship courses, are admitted to provide a fine test of golf. It is by virtue of their natural formation that they do so. The beauty of golf courses has suffered in the past from the creations of ugly and unimaginative design. Square, flat greens and geometrical bunkers have not only been an eyesore upon the whole landscape, but have detracted from the infinite variety of play which is the heritage of the game.

My reputation in the past has been based on the fact that I have endeavoured to conserve existing natural features, and where these are lacking to create formations in the spirit of nature herself.

In other words, while always keeping uppermost the provision of a splendid test of golf, I have striven to achieve beauty.

———•———

There is an extraordinary resemblance between what is now known as the camouflage of military earthworks and golf course construction.

The writer was fortunate during the war in being asked to give the demonstrations to members of the Army Council which were the foundation of, and led to the establishment of, the first school of camouflage.

These demonstrations were evolved from his experience as a golf course architect in the imitation of natural features.

Successful golf course construction and successful camouflage are almost entirely due to utilization of natural features to the fullest extent and to the construction of artificial ones indistinguishable from nature.

It is clear that if a gun emplacement or any other object of military importance is made indistinguishable from the most innocent looking feature on the landscape, it will escape the disagreeable attention of the enemy. And what can appear more innocent than the natural undulations of the ground? Therefore in camouflage, as in golf course construction, the ability to imitate natural undulations successfully is of special importance.

There are many other attributes in common between the successful golf architect and the camoufleur.

Both, if not actually artists, must have an artistic temperament, and have had an education in science.

Surprise is the most important thing in war, and by camouflage you are able to obtain this not only on the defense but in the attack.

In golf architecture and camouflage a knowledge of psychology is of enormous value. It enables one to judge what is likely to give pleasurable excitement to the golfer and confidence and improvement in *morale* to the soldier.

The writer feels most strongly that his experience in the Great War in visualizing and surveying miles of sites for fortifications in this country and abroad, in map reading, in the interpretation of aerial photographs, in drainage and labor saving problems, and particularly in the mental training of strategic camouflage and devising traps and surprises for the enemy, was by no means wasted even from a golf course point of view. The only man he has been successful in initiating rapidly into the mysteries of golf course architecture was not a golfer but an artist, and one of the greatest, if not the greatest, of experts on camouflage.

———

Aerial photography will become of enormous value in all kinds of surveying, town planning, the construction of golf courses, etc.

There are all sorts of details visible in an aerial photograph which are often omitted after the most careful survey in the ordinary way. The exact positions of every tree, hummock, natural bunker, tracks, hedges, ditches, etc., are well defined. The exact areas occupied by permanent pasture, grass grown for hay, crops, clumps of whins, rushes, etc., can all be distinguished in an aerial photograph.

These, combined with a good ordnance and geological drift-map, are of inestimable value, and in many cases would assist even the most expert golf architect to make such full use of all the natural features that thousands of pounds might ultimately be saved in reducing the acreage required and in minimizing the cost of labor, upkeep, etc.

*By A.W. Tillinghast:*

I emphasized the necessity of pulling out the slopes to the ratio of six feet to every foot of elevation (my invariable rule) and of BLENDING all. The word "blending" I use a great deal in my explanations and it proves to be a good one for my purposes.

———•———

I sometimes take my very life in my hands when I suggest that a certain tree happens to be spoiling a pretty good hole. The green committee chairman is like as not to glare at me as though I had recommended that he go home and murder his wife.

# CHAPTER 6

## Teeing Grounds

*"This placing of the tee shot, if not overdone, is one of the best features of modern golf course construction work." - H.S. Colt*

*By H.S. Colt:*

In making the different teeing grounds it will be possible to gain a little extra variety by playing the tee shot at different angles to the course; thus a teeing ground made at some thirty yards or so to the right or left of the one in front will very likely create additional interest in the round, and be better than one made exactly behind it.

---

A test of accuracy must also be provided for tee shots, and the player learn to take a line, and not just blaze away at right angles to the teeing ground. All who know the Old Course at St. Andrews will realize what I am attempting to explain, as their caddies have many a time told them to play on the College Church steeple or other well-known landmarks; indeed, a friend of mine even carries this to such an extreme that he told me on one occasion that, in playing the last tee shot of the round, he framed on the

"D" in the words "Grand Hotel" displayed in large letters on the building behind the 18th green. I am not quite sure whether that shot finished on the "H" or in the area steps of the houses on the right. In providing this test for accurate driving, a good sprinkling of lateral hazards is necessary. Heather is useful in this direction, and also long grass, but the latter should not take the form of the meadow just ready for the hay-cutting machine. A hayfield and golf never seem to me to go well together. The rough, sandy hummocks of a seaside links prove excellent side hazards. Then, again, the central bunker in the course itself forces a player to try to place his ball in a desired area. This placing of the tee shot, if not overdone, is one of the best features of modern golf course construction work; and it can also be easily enforced by the hazards near the green, so that they govern the tee shot even if there be no bunkers for that stroke.

### By A.W. Tillinghast:

I still observe the tendency to preserve pulpit-like, raised teeing grounds. The larger, natural looking teeing areas are to be found on most of our first-class courses today, but I still observe the relics of the dark ages on too many links.

# CHAPTER 7

## Through the Green

*"Narrow fairways bordered by long grass make bad golfers."* – Alister MacKenzie

*By Alister MacKenzie:*

An almost equally common delusion is that fairways should be flat. I quite agree that there is nothing worse than a fairway on a severe side slope, but, on the other hand, there are few things more monotonous than playing every shot from a dead flat fairway. The unobservant player never seems to realize that one of the chief charms of the best seaside links is the undulating fairways, such as those near the clubhouse at Deal, part of Sandwich, and most of the Old Course at St. Andrews, where the ground is a continual roll from the first tee to the last green, and where one never has the same shot to play twice; on these fairways one hardly ever has a level stance or a level lie. It is this that makes the variety of a seaside course, and variety is everything in golf.

If one considers St. Andrews hole by hole, it is surprising to find at how many of them the dominating and important incident is associated with an insignificant looking hollow or bank, often running obliquely to the line of your approach.

In constructing undulations of this kind on inland courses, it is well to make them with as much variety as possible, and in the direction you wish the player to go to keep the fairway comparatively flat, so as to encourage players to place their shots, and thus get in a favorable position for their next.

In this connection, plasticine is frequently used for making models of undulations. Plasticine is useful to teach the greenkeeper points in construction he would not otherwise understand—in fact, I believe, I was the first designer of golf courses to use it for this purpose. The 14th green at Alwoodley, which was the first one made there, was constructed from a model in plasticine. It has its disadvantages, however, as a course constructed entirely from models in plasticine has always an artificial appearance, and can never be done as cheaply as one in which the greenkeeper is allowed a comparatively free hand in modelling the undulations in such a manner that not only do they harmonize with their surroundings, but are constructed according to the various changes in the subsoil discovered whilst doing the work.

———◆◆◆———

It is an important thing in golf to make holes look much more difficult than they really are. People get more pleasure in doing a hole which looks almost impossible, and yet is not so difficult as it appears.

In this connection it may be pointed out that rough grass is of little interest as a hazard. It is frequently much more difficult than a fearsome-looking bunker or belt of whins or rushes, but it causes considerable annoyance in lost balls, and no one ever gets the same thrills in driving over a stretch of rough as over a fearsome-looking bunker, which in reality may not be so severe.

Narrow fairways bordered by long grass make bad golfers. They do so by destroying the harmony and continuity of the game, and in causing a stilted and cramped style by destroying all freedom of play.

There is no defined line between the fairways in the great schools of golf like St. Andrews or Hoylake.

It is a common error to cut the rough in straight lines. It should be cut in irregular, natural looking curves. The fairways should gradually widen out where a long drive goes; in this way a long driver is given a little more latitude in pulling and slicing.

Moreover, irregular curves assist a player in locating the exact position of a ball which has left the fairway and entered the rough.

*By H.S. Colt:*

For another purpose, undulations and hummocks are of great value "through the green," as they provide difficult stances and lies, without which no golf course can be said to be quite perfect. I well remember an argument upon this point which I had some little time back at Sunningdale. The course was looking its best, having been recently cut, and the turf was even and smooth. Although when adverse criticism occurs a secretary is always liable to take the bait, yet when there is by chance fulsome praise he is just as liable to object. And when someone came up to me and admired the state of the green, out of sheer contrariness I objected, and said that the lies were getting much too good. My friend would not agree on the ground that if a good shot had been made, the player was entitled to the best of everything. But this can be overdone, as what we want to do, amongst other things, is to extract the very best golf from a man, and nothing does this so much as difficult lies and difficult stances. After playing over links where you never get them, it is very hard to pick up a ball from a badly hanging lie, and it needs a lot of practice and skill to play the stroke successfully. This is generally the weakness of inland courses, and where they have been ploughed up and sown with seed, the surface has, in the past, been usually levelled at the same time, and a number of small interesting details removed.

## APPROACH SHOTS

*By H.S. Colt:*

Let us now consider the approach shots on a course, whether they be a short "pitch" with a mashie or a full shot with a brassie—in fact, all strokes when the putting green can be reached. Hazards, which would be perfectly fair for a short run-up, may be manifestly absurd for a full shot, as the greater the distance to be covered, the more latitude there must be for error. This creates the difficulty in designing interesting approach play for all classes of players, as all sorts of problems arise out of it. If a bunker be made at one spot for the long driver, it will be very likely unfair for the short player, and vice versa. One or two suggestions have been made previously on this point, when considering the tee shot, which may be useful now. There must always be a certain amount of conflict between the various classes of players. In the one case the ripe veteran must be occasionally sacrificed, and told that when the ground is soft and the wind in his teeth he must carry 300 yards or so in two shots or play short; and, on the other hand, the committee may occasionally have no pity for the slashing young player of twenty or so, and provide him with a pitfall when he hits an extra-long one under rather abnormal conditions. We have to accept this if we are to have interesting approach play for the vast majority of players under normal conditions.

The hazards applicable for the tee shot will be suitable for the full shot played in approaching the green, and one or two cross hazards giving a long carry will be acceptable to most people. No doubt at times it will mean playing short, and thus the benefit of an extra well hit drive will be lost, but one or two instances—I would not want more personally—of this class of stroke are advisable. It is not everyone who can pick up a close-lying ball from hard ground with a brassie and lash it over a big bunker.

If we are to have wing bunkers near the green, the antithesis of the foregoing, we can make the passage between narrower than for the drive, as a man should have more confidence in playing his second shot than his first. We do not, however, want to see them cut exactly opposite each other and at right angles to the course.

Now we come to the class of full approach shot which always appeals to me, one which is vitally affected by the line taken from the tee. The 10th hole at Sunningdale is a good instance of this. The bunker near the green is close to the hole, but, as the ground between rises, a long second shot is pulled up in time. To see that hole played well is to me always a treat, especially if the player knows on the tee that he cannot carry this bunker with his second stroke. He has to place his tee shot to the right, and then just shave past the bunker on the left with his second, and if the hole is cut on the upper portion of the regular green, just a shade of pull is an advantage. If he fears disaster and wants safety, he can obtain it at the expense of having a long run-up to lay dead for a four. A hole like that is perfectly fair for everyone—the short, the medium, and the long—and gives most excellent sport for all, besides being, under ordinary conditions, a really fine test of the game. It provides the very long carry for the man of great power, it furnishes the skilful and medium-length player with a chance of playing an exceptionally good one, and it constantly supplies a short pitch for all those who fail to reach the green in two shots, and also a fair amount of niblick work.

The 4th hole at Sandwich is another instance of a grand hole of the same type, although now possibly a little on the short side with the new balls. It required, at any rate, the same placing to the right of the tee shot to avoid the deep ravine on the left near the green. The drive is governed by the difficulties provided for the approach— the two hang together—as the player, when he stands on the teeing ground, is even then compelled to consider his second stroke. We need several holes of this description in our course. If anyone has to depend upon skill and judgment as against power alone, certainly penalize him if he fails to place his shot accurately. By all means give such a one an impossible carry; trap him in any way you like, and give him no quarter. But if he offend not, let us provide him in the general course of events with something possible and interesting, and not have only one rejoinder to his protest—"You can play short."

As the central and diagonal hazards have been dealt with already, we will now consider approach shots of shorter range than the full shot. Many think that the golfer who would be well-equipped in the matter of approach should be able to play three classes of strokes for such distances. He must be able to pitch high and stop quickly, to pitch-and-run, and to run-up, and thus the ground is covered in three distinct ways.

———————•••———————

Now consider the firm half-shot of such players as Bob Martin with his cleek, or Andrew Kirkaldy and J.H. Taylor with their driving mashies, played with but little effort and very likely in the teeth of a strong wind. And if we are ambitious in trying to provide opportunities for testing the abilities of the real artist in approach play—and there are few more interesting things in golf than such an attempt—we shall probably find that we need further materials than bunkers and hazards of the ordinary description. If we had to depend alone upon them, the course would be either too easy for the championship player or too hard for the ordinary one. There are two classes of difficulties which are most useful for our purpose—plateau greens and "hummocky" ground. The vast majority of links need both badly. A narrow plateau for a green, or a few hummocks in front of one, will very likely cause just as much trouble and amusement to a player as a gaping chasm stretching right across the course. Without doubt, we want bunkers to pitch over; but, for the reasons previously mentioned, we cannot rely entirely upon them for creating interesting and testing approach play.

As an instance of a good plateau green, take the 12th hole at St. Andrews. There is, certainly, the small pot bunker some fifty yards or so in front of the green, but that is never the real difficulty in getting close to the pin. It is the narrow plateau and the two shoulders on each side, more particularly that on the left. The man who can only play the high pitching shot with his mashie has not much chance of a putt for a three here. Or for a longer approach shot, take the 16th hole on the same course, and watch Andrew Kirkaldy play it, and we shall most probably see him use a straight-faced iron club with a satisfactory result. And, again, as an instance of a hummock, let us take the 4th hole on the same course. Have we not all been bothered by it on innumerable occasions? It has proved of just as much value for the purposes of a hazard to make us try to play the right class of shot as the deepest bunker in existence.

———————•—————

The high pitch shot must not be left out of consideration, as we want as many of them as possible in the course; and not only the pitch shot with a mashie, but also an instance here and there of the high stopping shot with the mid-spoon. In fact, we want examples of every class and description of stroke to be played at some time or another during the round.

———————•—————

It is now a case of reverting occasionally to a class of hole which used to exist when golf courses had not been almost reduced to standardization. I refer to the occasion when a player would take a short club off the tee so as to arrive at a spot from which a long, full second shot could be played with more advantage than by reversing the order of strokes. Such a scheme will appeal to those who favor not only straight hitting off the tee, but also the placing of the tee shot in the correct position so far as length is concerned. We must not have many of these tee shots, as otherwise a premium is likely to be placed on short driving. Ground should be selected for this sort of hole, and also for a dogleg hole, which presents some natural features insisting upon or emphasizing the class of shot which we are trying to develop; otherwise the effect will be labored and artificial.

# CHAPTER 8

————◦————

# Hazards

*"It is a matter of record that I have condemned nearly eight thousand sand traps." – A.W. Tillinghast*

*By Alister MacKenzie:*

Most of the remaining principles depend on the proper disposition of hazards, and I have a rather wider definition of hazards than is given by the rules of golf committee. As a minor kind of hazard, undulating ground, hummocks, hollows, etc., might be included.

Most golfers have an entirely erroneous view of the real object of hazards. The majority of them simply look upon hazards as a means of punishing a bad shot, when their real object is to make the game interesting.

————◦————

It is much too large a subject to go into the question of the placing of hazards, but I would like to emphasize a fundamental principle. It is that, as already pointed out, no hazard is unfair wherever it is placed.

A hazard placed in the exact position where a player would naturally go is frequently the most interesting situation, as then a special effort is needed to get over or avoid it.

———————●———————

One of the objects in placing hazards is to give the players as much pleasurable excitement as possible. On many inland courses there is not a thrill on the whole round, and yet on some of the championship courses one rarely takes a club out of the bag without having an interesting shot to play. This particularly applies to the Old Course at St. Andrews, and is one of the reasons why it always retains its popularity with all classes of players. It is quite true that even this course is condemned by some, but this may be due to the fact that they have not brains enough, or have not played on it long enough, to appreciate its many virtues.

There are some leading players who honestly dislike the dramatic element in golf. They hate anything that is likely to interfere with a constant succession of threes and fours. They look upon everything in the "card and pencil" spirit. The average club member on the other hand is a keen sportsman, he looks upon golf in the "spirit of adventure," and that is why St. Andrews and courses modelled on similar ideals appeal to him.

No one would pretend that the Old Course at St. Andrews is perfect: It has its disadvantages, particularly in the absence of long carries from the tee, and in its blind bunkers, but no links in the world grows upon all classes of players in the same manner. The longer one plays there the keener one gets, and this is a much truer test of a good course than one which pleases at first and is boring later on.

A good golf course is like good music or good anything else; it is not necessarily a course which appeals the first time one plays over it, but one which grows on the player the more frequently he visits it.

St. Andrews is a standing example of the possibility of making a course which is pleasurable to all classes of golfers, not only to the thirty handicap players, but to the plus fourteen man, if there ever was or will be such a person.

It is an interesting fact that few hazards are of any interest which are out of what is known among medical men as the direct field of vision. This does not extend much farther than ten to twenty yards on either side of the direct line to the hole. Hazards placed outside this limit are usually of little interest, but simply act as a source of irritation.

Hazards should be placed with an object, and none should be made which has not some influence on the line of play to the hole.

*By H.S. Colt:*

There is one class of hazard which has appealed to me very greatly for the last three or four years—the diagonal hazard. We do not want this, however, overdone and to see it everywhere, whatever the nature of the ground. But if the latter is suitable, it provides sport for everyone, and the subsequent scheme of a hole can give advantage to the one who bites off the biggest slice of the hazard. The 5th hole at Swinley Forest, and also the 5th hole at Sunningdale, especially with the green now extended to the right, are examples.

We can have great variety in the character of the difficulties provided for the delectation of the golfer, and if we go one step further, we can have variety in each class of hazard. The shape and nature of bunkers can be varied with immense advantage. How often do we see a delightful landscape spoilt by the creation of a number of symmetrical pots, or banks, or humps, made apparently at so much a dozen! And this landscape might have been improved, and made still more pleasing to the eye, by planting judiciously off the course irregular clumps of whins, or broom, or rough grasses, or possibly small birch trees and Scotch firs. If we have to make bunkers—and no doubt they will be necessary—we can in great measure conceal their artificiality, and in any event we need not make them of a certain stereotyped pattern. Some can be sunk without banks; some can have rough banks added to them; some can be sand and some rough grass; some can be in the nature of rough, irregular, wide grass ditches, and so on. If they are sunk, then a little treatment of the ground prior to their commencement will be a help in our attempt to remove the stain of artificiality. The ground can be gradually sloped down to the proposed level of the bottom of the hazard. A small bunker with a draw into it is often more serviceable than a large sandy waste. But wherever possible let us take advantage of a rise in the ground for a bank or of a hollow for a pot. Nature will often provide us with a small feature which will work in successfully with the scheme for a good hole.

Further, the margins of the course can in many cases be allowed to provide in great measure the difficulties for the round. If we have all our margins cut so as to give the impression of the use of the measuring rod and garden line, we shall have a course which will satisfy only the strictly golfing portion of a man's nature, and deprive him of considerable pleasure from playing the game amidst pleasing surroundings. The margins of the course can be made so as to form a bay here and a promontory there, and these will be of use as difficulties in the play of the various holes.

It is a great pleasure to some of us to break up the horrible regularity so often met with on inland links.

## BUNKERS

*By Alister MacKenzie:*

On many courses there are far too many bunkers: The sides of the fairways are riddled with them, and many of these courses would be equally interesting if half of the bunkers were turfed over as grassy hollows.

It is often possible to make a hole sufficiently interesting with one or two bunkers at the most.

———•———

Bunkers on an inland course should, as a rule, be made in the opposite way to what is customary. At the present time most bunkers have the hollows sanded and the banks turfed. It is suggested that you get a much more natural appearance if the hollows are partly turfed over and the hummocks sanded. This has the following advantages: The appearance is much more like a seaside course; the sand being above the level of the ground, always remains dry. The contrast between white or yellow sand and the grass helps one to judge distances much more accurately, and enables the ball to be found more easily, and the great disadvantage and expense of scything the long grass on the hummocks to prevent lost balls is done away with.

Ordinary bunkers are, as a rule, made in quite the wrong way. The face is usually too upright and the ball gets into an unplayable position under the face. The bottom of the bank of a bunker should have a considerable slope, so that a ball always rolls to the middle; the top of a bunker may, as it usually does in nature, be made to overhang a little so as to prevent a topped ball running through it.

Experience gained in the imitation of natural slopes in bunker making was ultimately responsible for saving tens of thousands of pounds in revetting material in the Great War.

---

Hazards are usually placed too far away from the greens they are intended to guard; they should be placed immediately on the edge of the greens, and then (particularly if they are in the form of smooth hillocks and hollows) the player who is wide of them has an extremely difficult pitch, and is frequently worse off than the man who is in them.

A bunker eating into a green is by far the most equitable way of giving a golfer full advantage for accurate play. It not only penalizes the man who is in it, but everyone who is wide of it. For example, a player who is in the road bunker at the 17th at St. Andrews may, with a good dunch shot, get out and lie dead, but few can pitch over it so accurately that they do so. A bunker, similarly placed to the road bunker, may be made to accentuate this distinction; it may be constructed with so much slope that on occasions it can be putted out of.

# CHAPTER 9

## Greens and Greenkeeping

*"Eighteen flat greens are to me an abomination, and the pleasantly undulating green which provides 'possible' putting even in a dry summer is far preferable."*
*– H.S. Colt*

*By Alister MacKenzie:*

It used to be a common fallacy that greens should be made dead flat. Even on some of the best golf courses at the present day you find them made like croquet lawns. There has been somewhat of a reaction lately against undulating greens, but this, I believe, is entirely due to the fact that the undulations have been made of a wrong character, either composed of finicky little humps or of the ridge and furrow type. Natural undulations are the exact opposite to the artificial ridge and furrow. The latter has a narrow hollow, and a broad ridge, whereas the former has a large, bold, sweeping hollow, and a narrow ridge.

------

In constructing natural looking undulations, one should attempt to study the manner in which those among the sand dunes are formed. These are fashioned by the wind blowing up the sand in the form of waves, which become gradually turfed over in the course of time. Natural undulations are, therefore, of a similar shape to the waves one sees by the seashore, and are of all kinds of shapes and sizes, but are characterized by the fact that the hollows between the waves are broader than the waves themselves.

If undulations are made of this kind, then there are always plenty of comparatively flat places where the greenkeeper can put the flag, and there should never be any necessity to cut the hole on a slope.

A test of a good undulation is that it should be easy to use the mowing machine over it.

If undulations are made of the kind I describe, it is hardly possible to make them too large or too bold.

Perhaps the most aggravating type of undulation is the finicky little hump or side slope which you don't see until after you have missed your putt, and then begin to wonder why it has not gone in the hole.

## By H.S. Colt:

[On green placement] Personally, I like to select a ridge or a low plateau in preference to a hollow. The green is obviously more visible to the player, which is a feature after which I strive. And if we can select a wide hog's back for the purpose, we shall not need much, if any, artificial help in the nature of bunkers. Still I would not by any means wish to eliminate altogether the punch-bowl green from a course, as, although weak from the point of view of a test of skill, it is delightful in other respects. Eighteen flat greens are to me an abomination, and the pleasantly undulating green which provides "possible" putting even in a dry summer is far preferable. On the other hand, two or three examples of the flat green are an advantage.

—————— • • ——————

In conclusion, I can say that I have made no attempt to prescribe for the size of greens or tees, for the width or length of the various holes, for the depth or shape of the bunkers, as it is my firm conviction that the less said on these subjects the better. I have met with so many "thirty-by-thirties" in putting greens, "ten-by-tens" in tees, and so much similarity in bunkers, that I am sick to death of them. Immediately we attempt to standardize sizes, shapes, and distances we lose more than half the pleasure of the game. Too much stress cannot be laid upon the necessity of seeing and using the natural features present on each course to the fullest possible extent. It is only by doing this and selecting them judiciously for their special purposes that we can arrive at the success at which we aim. We must seize upon them with a grasping hand, and if possible not let one of them escape us. If perchance they be numerous and varied in character, then we shall have an opportunity of constructing a course which will give a real and genuine pleasure to all to play over, whatever their skill in the game may be.

## By A. W. Tillinghast:

Let me state here that when I encounter those who are used to extremely large greens I do not try to tear them away from their predilections, except where the great areas rob greens, reached by short shots, of any virtue. It is well-known that I always have favored the comparatively smaller and closely guarded green, but I certainly refrained from injecting my personal feelings into the pictures where I sense that the contrary method has been favored. I find the courses, where the large greens have been fancied, are cutting them down in size gradually as their futility is recognized.

## GREENKEEPING

*By Alister MacKenzie:*

A common mistake in greenkeeping is to imagine that because one form of treatment benefits one course, that it will necessarily benefit another.

The greenkeeper should have sufficient knowledge of chemistry and botany to be able to tell exactly what form of treatment is most likely to benefit his greens.

For example, the ordinary artificial manure sold by some seed merchants for golf courses consists of a mixture of three parts of superphosphate of lime, one part each sulphate of ammonia and sulphate of potash, and one-tenth part of sulphate of iron. If no weeds are present, the sulphate of iron may be omitted from the mixture; if daisies are present, the sulphate of ammonia should be increased; if clover is present, the potash and lime should be lessened in quantity; if the turf is sour, or if sorrel is present, the sulphate of ammonia should be lessened, and lime used as a separate dressing.

Farmyard manure should not, as a rule, be used as a surface dressing on golf courses: It is much too likely to encourage weeds and worms.

Something of the nature of Peruvian guano, fish guano, meat guano, malt culms, or dried blood, together with artificials, should be used in its place. If humus is necessary, it may be added in the form of peat moss litter, minced seaweed, etc., and the box should seldom be used on the mowing machines.

It must be borne in mind that the turf required on a golf course is entirely different to that required from a farming point of view.

It is now an absolutely exploded fallacy that worms are of any use on a golf course; they should be got rid of by the use of charcoal obtained from steel furnaces: Ordinary wood charcoal is almost useless. Charcoal in this form acts mechanically, owing to the small sharp pieces of steel attached to it: It scratches the worms and prevents them getting through.

Worm-killers, especially consisting of Mowrah meal, are of great value in destroying worms.

It is a mistake to consider that worm-killers, unless mixed with an artificial manure, have any manurial value. The greenkeeper will tell you that after the application, the grass has come up much greener. That is due to the fact that the worms are no longer discoloring it by crawling over it with their slimy bodies.

---

A common mistake is not to mow greens during the winter months. I have not the slightest doubt that mowing greens during the winter months is beneficial to them: It keeps the grass from becoming coarse.

On those Scotch courses where the greens are so good all through the winter, are not the rabbits mowing the greens all through the winter months?

Are the knives of the mowing machine any more likely to do the grass harm than the teeth of the rabbits?

It is a common mistake in sowing a green not to use a sufficient quantity of seed. The ground should always be thoroughly prepared and manured according to the chemical composition of the soil; then as much as five or six bushels of seed per green can be sown to advantage.

Mixtures of grass seeds may be sold consisting of a considerable proportion of seeds which do not germinate, and are not likely to do so on ordinary soils. Unscrupulous seed merchants may undercut the more honest ones in this way. Three bushels of the best seeds will go further than six containing a large proportion of varieties which are not likely to germinate.

———— •◦• ————

My last principle is one which particularly affects the greenkeeper: The course should be perfect all the year round.

It is quite a prevalent idea that courses on a clay subsoil can never be made into good winter links. It does not matter so much, as might be expected, what the subsoil is like, provided it is well drained and the turf on the top is of the right texture. Muddy courses are entirely due to insufficient drainage, worms, and the wrong kind of turf.

Worms can be got rid of and the right kind of turf encouraged by adopting modern methods of greenkeeping. Many examples of what can be done in converting really bad winter courses into good ones can be seen in the North. Surface drainage, such as mole draining, gets rid of worms by making the land so dry that they cannot work.

# CHAPTER 10

## Ideal Holes

*"If these bunkers only looked as terrifying and formidable as they really are, what thrills one would get in playing this hole! What pleasurable excitement there would be in seeing one's second shot sailing over Hell!" – Alister MacKenzie*

*By Alister MacKenzie:*

There are few problems more difficult to solve than the problem of what exactly constitutes an ideal hole. The ideal hole is surely one that affords the greatest pleasure to the greatest number, gives the fullest advantage for accurate play, stimulates players to improve their game, and never becomes monotonous.

The real practical test is its popularity, and here again we are up against another difficulty. Does the average player really know what he likes himself? One often hears the same player expressing totally divergent opinions about the same hole. When he plays it successfully, it is everything that is good, and when unsuccessful it is everything that is bad. It frequently happens that the best holes give rise to the most bitter controversy. It is largely a question of the spirit in which the problem is approached.

Does the player look upon it from the "card and pencil" point of view and condemn anything that has disturbed his steady series of threes and fours, or does he approach the question in the "spirit of adventure" of the true sportsman?

There are well-known players who invariably condemn any hole they have taken over six for, and if by any chance they ever reach double figures, words fail them to describe in adequate language what they think of that particular hole.

It does not by any means follow that when a player condemns a hole in particularly vigorous language he really dislikes it. It may be a source of pleasure to his subconscious mind. Although condemning it, he may be longing to play it again so as to conquer its difficulties.

Who is to judge what is an ideal hole? Is it one of our leading players, or any golfer who simply looks upon it from his own point of view? I have known of an open champion expressing his opinion that a certain course was superior to any in Britain. As far as this particular course is concerned, it is generally admitted by amateurs that, although the turf and natural advantages were excellent, it had not a single hole of any real merit. The local committee were also of opinion that it was monotonous and lacking in real interest, and had decided to have it entirely remodeled, before this world renowned open champion persuaded them to change their minds by expressing such strong views in its favor.

There are, unfortunately, many leading players who wish a course to be designed so that it will favor their own play and will not even punish their indifferent shots, but will put any one below their particular standard out of the running altogether.

There are many leading players who condemn the strategic aspect of golf. They only see one line to the hole, and that is usually the direct one. They cannot see why they should, as in doglegged holes, be ever compelled to play to one or other side of the direct line. A bunker in the direct line at the distance of their long drives is invariably condemned by them, because they do not realize that the correct line is to one or other side of it. Why should not even an open champion occasionally have a shot that the long-handicap man is frequently compelled to play?

Should a course or hole be ideal from a medal or match playing point of view? If it is necessary to draw any distinction between the two, there can be little doubt that match play should always have prior claim. Nine out of ten games on most good courses are played in matches and not for medals. The true test of a hole is, then, its value in match play.

The majority of golfers are agreed, I think, that an ideal hole should be a difficult one. It is true there are some who would have it difficult for everyone except themselves. These, who usually belong to the pot-hunting fraternity, may be left out of consideration. It is the successful negotiation of difficulties, or apparent ones, which gives rise to pleasurable excitement and makes a hole interesting.

What kind of difficulties make interesting golf?

We can, I think, eliminate difficulties consisting of long grass, narrow fairways, and small greens, because of the annoyance and irritation caused by searching for lost balls, the disturbance of the harmony and continuity of the game, the consequent loss of freedom of swing, and the production of bad players.

We can also eliminate blind greens, blind bunkers, and blind approaches. The greater the experience the writer has of designing golf courses, the more certain he is that blindness of all kinds should be avoided. The only form of blindness that should ever be permitted is the full shot up to a green whose position is accurately located by surrounding sand hills. Even in a hole of this kind, it is not the blindness that is interesting, but the visibility of the surrounding sand hills. At the Maiden hole at Sandwich, it was the grandeur and the impressiveness of the Maiden that made it a good hole, and not the blindness of the green.

The difficulties that make a hole really interesting are usually those in which a great advantage can be gained in successfully accomplishing heroic carries over hazards of an impressive appearance, or in taking great risks in placing a shot so as to gain a big advantage for the next. Successfully carrying or skirting a bunker of an alarming or impressive appearance is always a source of satisfaction to the golfer, and yet it is hazards of this description which so often give rise to criticism by the unsuccessful player. At first sight he looks upon it as grossly unfair that, of two shots within a few inches of each other, the one should be hopelessly buried in a bunker and the other should be in an ideal position.

However, on further consideration he will realize that, as in doglegged holes, this is the chief characteristic of all good holes.

Holes of this description not only cater for great judgment, but great skill: A man who has such confidence that he can place his ball within a few feet of his objective gains a big advantage over a faint-hearted opponent who dare not take similar risks. On a course, with holes of this kind, match play becomes of intense interest.

In a perfect hole the surface of not only the green, but the approach to it, should be visible. It is difficult, or even impossible, to judge an approach accurately unless the ground which the ball pitches on can be seen. It also gives great pleasure (or sometimes pain) to see the result of one's shot.

In an ideal hole, the turf should be as perfect as possible and the approaches should have the same consistency as the greens, but it is by no means advisable to avoid entirely bad lies or irregular stances. There is not only much skill required, but an improvement of one's game results in occasionally having to play out of a cupped lie, or from an uneven stance. There are few things more monotonous than always playing from a dead flat fairway.

In an ideal long hole, there should not only be a big advantage from successfully negotiating a long carry for the tee shot, but the longer the drive, the greater the advantage should be. A shorter driver should also, by extreme accuracy, be able to gain an advantage over a long hitting but less accurate opponent.

An ideal hole should provide an infinite variety of shots according to the varying positions of the tee, the situation of the flag, the direction and strength of the wind, etc. It should also at times give full advantage for the voluntary pull or slice, one of the most finished shots in golf, and one that few champions are able to carry out with any great degree of accuracy.

Should an ideal hole be ideal for the plus, scratch, or long-handicap player? As players of all handicaps play golf, a hole should as far as possible be ideal for all classes. There are many famous holes, such as the Cardinal, which are by no means ideal, as in an ideal hole there should always be an alternative route open to the weaker player.

————————

Are there any ideal holes in existence at the present moment?

I think the 11th (the short hole coming in at St. Andrews) may be considered so. Under certain conditions, it is extremely difficult for even the best player that ever breathed, especially if he is attempting to get a two, but at the same time an inferior player may get a four if he plays his own game exceptionally well. It has been suggested that the mere fact that it is possible to putt the whole length is an objection to it. No doubt the timid golfer can play the hole in this way, but he will lose strokes by avoiding risks. Even if an expert putter holes out in four strokes once in three times, he can consider himself lucky. I do not know of a solitary example of a player achieving success in an important match by this means. If a cross bunker were constructed at this hole, it would become appreciably diminished in interest in consequence. The narrow entrance and the subtle slopes have all the advantages of a cross bunker without making it impossible for the long-handicap man. These contentions are borne out by those attempts that have been made to copy and improve on the hole by a cross bunker.

There are few, if any, other ideal short holes in existence. The 7th and 14th on the Eden Course at St. Andrews are remarkably fine holes, especially as they have to a great extent been artificially created. At the present moment the gorse in places is somewhat near both greens, but this can easily be rectified, and the architect, Mr. H.S. Colt, was wise in not removing too many whins in the first instance, as, if once removed, they cannot be replaced.

Another good example is the 8th at Moortown (formerly 17th, or, as it is known locally, Gibraltar). Its length is 170 yards, and it has been entirely artificially created at the small cost of thirty-five pounds.

The green has been constructed on a slight slope. The soil has been removed from the lower portion of the slope to make the bunkers and to bank up the green. The natural slope has been retained at the entrance to the green, and, like the 11th at St. Andrews, it is these subtle slopes which lead a ball which has not been correctly hit, into the adjacent bunkers, and in reality have very much the same effect as a cross bunker without the hardship to the long-handicap player.

The hole also shares with the 11th at St. Andrews the necessity for an infinite variety of shots according to varying conditions of wind, flag position, etc., One day it is a comparatively easy pitch with a mashie, normally it is a straight iron shot, sometimes a full shot with a trace of pull is required, and, again, it is necessary to slice so that one's ball is held up against the slope of the hill.

The green is delightfully picturesque. It is extremely visible against a background of fir trees—it stands up and looks at you.

The contrast between the vivid green of the grass, the dark green of the firs, the whiteness of the sand, the purple heather, and a vivid background of rhododendrons, combined with the natural appearance and extreme boldness of the contours, gives one a picture probably unsurpassed by anything of a similar kind in nature.

It is not only a delightful hole to see, which at any rate appeals subconsciously to the dullest of minds, but it is equally delightful to play. It is less difficult than it appears. You feel you are taking your life in your hands, and it therefore appeals, as Mr. Bernard Darwin says, to the "spirit of adventure"—yet a well-played shot always gets its due reward.

There are few, if any, ideal two- or three-shot holes in existence. Some of those coming in at St. Andrews are almost, but not quite, perfect.

The 16th (Corner of the Dyke) hole at St. Andrews is almost ideal for its length (338 yards). It was a particularly good hole at the time of the guttie ball, and is so today for a short driver, like the writer.

As in the majority of good holes, it is the subtlety of the slopes that makes it so.

The green is tilted up slightly from right to left, and it would be a better hole still if the inclination were greater. It is also guarded by Grant's and the Wig Bunkers on the left-hand side, so that the approach from the right is easy, as all the slopes assist the players, and the approach from the left is exceedingly difficult.

The point about the hole is that it is so difficult to get into the best position to approach the green, because of the proximity of the Principal's Nose Bunker to the railway, and the difficulty of placing one's tee shot in such a small space with all the slopes leading to the bunker. On the other hand, there is a perfectly easy route free from all risk to the left of the Principal's Nose, but the player in all probability loses a stroke by taking it.

The 14th and 17th holes at St. Andrews are excellent holes, full of dramatic incident in match play.

The 14th hole is probably the best hole of its length in existence. Here, again, the hole is made by the slope of the green. There is a most marked tilt up from left to right, so much that it is impossible to approach near the hole from the right. It is slopes of this kind which are so often overlooked in designing a golf course, and it is one of the most difficult things imaginable to construct them really well; but it is subtleties of this nature which make all the difference between a good course and a bad one.

At the 14th hole at St. Andrews, this tilt of the green has a considerable influence on the tee shot 530 yards away. Some years ago there were four of us playing four ball matches nearly every day for a month. We, according to our own judgment, attempted to play this hole in four different ways. A played his tee shot well away to the left of the Beardies on to the low ground below the Elysian Fields, so as to place his second in a favorable position for his approach. B, who was a long driver, attempted to carry the Beardies with his drive, Hell with his second, and run-up his third. C, who was a short but fairly accurate hitter, attempted to pinch the Beardies as near as he dare, and then played his second well away to the left, so as to play against the slope of the green for his third. D took what was apparently the straightforward route along the large broad plateau of the Elysian Fields, and eventually landed in Hell or Perdition every time: He invariably lost the hole.

This hole is very nearly ideal, but would be better still if the lie of the land were such that the Beardies, the Crescent, the Kitchen, and Hell Bunkers were visible and impressive looking. If these bunkers only looked as terrifying and formidable as they really are, what thrills one would get in playing this hole! What pleasurable excitement there would be in seeing one's second shot sailing over Hell!

It may be, however, that it is just as well these bunkers are blind. If they had been visible, although in reality they would have been much fairer, there would have been so many players crying out that it was most unfair that bunkers should be placed in the exact position where perfect shots go; that it was most iniquitous to have a hazard like the Beardies 180 yards from the tee exactly in the line for the hole; that the carry over Hell for the second shot is over 400 yards from the tee; and that the only way to play the hole was along the fairway to the 5th, etc.

As these bunkers are blind, players do not notice these things, and the lives of the green committee are saved.

The 17th hole at St. Andrews is almost too well-known to need description—it is probably the most noted hole in the world. Although so difficult, it is by no means impossible for the long-handicap player, for he can go pottering along, steering wide of all hazards, and losing strokes because he refuses to take any risks.

At this hole, once more, it is the slopes that give so much character to the hole.

Even for the tee shot there is a ridge immediately beyond the corner of the station master's garden which kicks your ball away from the hole if you pitch to the left of it, and towards the hole if you pitch to the right—in fact, an extra yard or two over the corner makes all the difference in getting into a favorable position for the second shot. There are also hillocks and ridges down the right-hand side, all forcing an inaccurately placed shot into an unfavorable position for the approach.

I often think that the hole would be more interesting without the Scholar's Bunker—the latter prevents a badly hit second getting into the danger zone. If it were not there, one would much more frequently be forced to play the sporting approach to the green with the road bunker intervening. It is this road bunker, with the slopes leading a ball to it, which makes this hole of such intense interest. Notwithstanding the abuse showered on it, this bunker has done more to sustain the popularity of St. Andrews than any feature on the course.

During the last few years there have been many good inland courses constructed. Several of these, such as Swinley Forest, St. George's Hill, Sunningdale, Alwoodley, Moortown, Ganton, etc., have some excellent long holes.

At Alwoodley, two of the doglegged holes, the 8th and 15th, are particularly good examples. The 8th is played from right to left and the 15th from left to right. In each case the green has been constructed with a marked side slope, so that the nearer the golfer plays to the angle of the dogleg, the greater the slope favors him.

In 1914, the writer designed an ideal two-shot hole which won the first prize in a competition for *Golfing Architecture*, promoted by *Country Life*.

In designing it, he attempted to produce an ideal hole among perfect surroundings, and what could be more perfect than sand dunes by the seashore!

The hole is 420 yards long from the ordinary and 450 yards from the Medal Tee.

An effort has been made to produce the old type of golf, in which a player has no fixed line to the hole, but has to use his own judgment in playing it, according to varying conditions of wind, etc.

The green is guarded by bunkers and a large hillock (twenty feet high) on the right of the approach, and is also tilted upwards from left to right and from the front to the back, so that the approach from the left is an easy one, and from the right necessitates such a difficult pitch that the player is likely to overrun the green into the bunker beyond.

There are five possible routes to the hole, and the choice of the player must vary from day to day, according to his length of drive, the state of the weather, etc.

It caters for all classes of players—even the absolute beginner can take No. 5 line. He loses strokes not by getting into bunkers, but by avoiding risks, and probably takes five, or at least four, to reach the green in consequence; nevertheless he enjoys his game, and not being disheartened, he improves, until finally he may be able to achieve the boldest line of all, and drive a fine ball straight to the hole.

He who takes the left-hand road by way of the island can also get home in two; he has a shorter carry, but has to make up for this by extreme accuracy.

*By H.S. Colt:*

A dogleg hole, like the first one at Hoylake, is to me one of the finest for an accurate test of the game. The player who can place his tee shot just past the Corner of the Dyke gains a big advantage there. And, again, in the old days at St. Andrews, before the rubber-cored ball was introduced, the man who could place his tee shot at the 17th hole between the corner of the wall and the bunker on the left was in a very enviable position compared with an opponent who had driven wide to the left.

# CHAPTER 11

## The Construction Process

*"The plagues of Egypt seem but slight evils in comparison with the trials sometimes experienced by the keen and anxious greenkeeper." – H.S. Colt*

*By Alister MacKenzie:*

The chief items in the construction of a golf course are the following:

1. Carting
2. Labor
3. Drainage
4. Seeding
5. Turfing
6. Manures
7. Sand

### CARTING

The cost of carting can often be reduced to a minimum by using a little thought in the work. The stone from stone walls, rocks, the turf from turf walls, or soil taken out of excavations should never be carted away: They can always be used for raising a neighboring green in the form of a plateau, or in making hummocks or large undulations indistinguishable from the natural ones which are so delightful on seaside courses. It is rarely necessary to cart soil from a distance for the purpose of making a hummock or a green. It is much more economical to remove a sufficient area of turf from and around the site of an intended hummock or green, and utilize the soil removed from the area around the hummock for this purpose. This is a double advantage. The surrounding ground is lowered as the hummock is raised, and makes the hummock appear higher, and at the same time it is made to merge imperceptibly into the surrounding hollow or hollows, and has a much more natural appearance. A hollow removed from the front of the green has the effect of making the green appear as if it were raised upon a plateau, and this is still further accentuated if the soil removed is also used to build up the green.

Similarly, the green and the bunkers guarding it should all be made at the same time; the soil moved in making the bunkers can then be utilized in the formation of the green. It was in former years considered imprudent to construct bunkers until the experience of playing revealed the proper position, but since those days our knowledge of greenkeeping has advanced. An expert can judge by the character of the grasses and the nature of the undulations the amount of run which the ball is likely to get, and this knowledge, combined with actual measurements, gives more information than it is possible to gain by playing. Perhaps the most important reason why the architect's scheme should be completed in the first instance is that bunkers are hardly ever placed in the right position afterwards. It is difficult to find a member of a green committee who is not subconsciously prejudiced against placing a bunker where he is likely to get trapped himself.

After carting, there is usually a considerable amount of labor necessary to obliterate the tracks. Carting should, when possible, be done when the ground is hard, in dry weather or during frost. Carts should not be allowed to wander about all over the place, but should be made to keep in one track. It is often advisable to remove the turf previous to carting, and relay it after the carting is finished. Carts can sometimes be replaced with advantage by sledges with flat-bottomed runners.

## LABOR

By introducing labor-saving machinery, we have recently been getting better results at less than pre-war cost. If work on a large scale is being done, the steam navvy or grab might be tried for excavating and making hummocks, etc.; traction engines are useful in uprooting small trees, and larger ones can, with advantage, be blown up by dynamite. I recently used blasting charges for the purpose of assisting to make bunkers. An article in one of the Sheffield papers somewhat humorously stated that this was not the first occasion Dr. MacKenzie's bunkers had been "blasted."

Trolleys on rails are frequently used to save carting or barrows.

The two machines which are found of the greatest value in saving labor are the turf-cutting machine and the American scraper or scoop—the former made from designs by the writer. It will cut an acre of sod in an afternoon, and, moreover, cuts them of a more even thickness than by hand. This machine is worked by two horses like a plough. One or two clubs have condemned it without a fair trial, and on inquiry I have usually found that the weather was too dry, the grass too long, the blades had not been set properly, or that it had been used by a man who had had no previous experience in working one. It has been used by scores of clubs with a great deal of success. At Moortown, we sodded over twenty acres of sour heath land with it. The cost of this amounted to little compared with sowing, as we were able to remove the sod from a neighboring field. Sowing would have cost at least twice as much, as there were no signs of even a blade of grass on most of the land, and no sowing was likely to be successful without lime and manuring, and carting a tremendous quantity of soil so as to form a seedbed. The results have been infinitely better and quicker than sowing at the rate of even twelve bushels of the best grass seeds to the acre.

The scraper is worked by a horse or two horses, and is particularly useful for excavating light soil, but can even be used on heavy land if each layer is ploughed before the scraper is used. The scraper is shaped like a large shovel, the handles are raised, and the horse pulls and it digs into the ground until it is full; the handles are then depressed and the horse pulls it along to the required situation; it is then tipped up, and the horse returns for another load. One horse and two men by this means can do the work of a score of men working in the ordinary way with wheelbarrows. In making hollows and hummocks it has an additional advantage in that it gives them automatically a natural appearance, and at the same time the horse in climbing up to the top of the hump compresses the soil, and it does not sink so much afterwards.

The scraper has been used with considerable success at Castletown (Isle of Man), Wheatley Park (Doncaster), and Grange-over-Sands, among other courses.

It is important in constructing a new, or altering an old course, to get the work done as quickly as possible: If the work is done gradually, the sod lies about for some time and is sometimes ruined. Most of the work should be done during October and November, before the frosts commence: Good methods of organization should prevent men being unemployed during frost. If the greens, drains, and sites of bunkers are previously pared, and the sod allowed to lie, then even though frost sets in, the sod may be removed and a certain amount of excavation can still be proceeded with. Sand, soil, and manures may be carted, hedges stubbed up, and trees removed during frost.

## DRAINAGE

It is advisable to drain golfing land much more thoroughly and efficiently than ordinary farm land, but, on the other hand, by exercising a little thought it can be done much more cheaply. For the purpose of golf it is not only unnecessary to drain as deeply as is customary for agricultural purposes, but it is much cheaper and more satisfactory to adopt a system of shallow drains.

On a golf course, there is never any necessity to make allowance for the possibility of subsoil ploughing; the drains can therefore be kept near the surface. The great thing to bear in mind in draining is that the water stratum must be tapped. On heavy clay land, it is absurd to put drains in the middle of the clay, unless the whole of the trench is filled with clinkers or other porous material, and this is needlessly expensive. Drains may at times be placed in a groove on the surface of the clay. On land of this description, drains may often be placed with advantage at as shallow a depth as from six to twelve inches. It should be unnecessary to state that no effort should be spared to see that there is sufficient fall, and for the purpose of ensuring this, it is often necessary to take the levels. Sufficient thought is rarely given to drainage. The site of the main drains and the whole scheme of drainage should be very carefully studied, and it is of special importance to take into consideration the nature of the subsoil and position of the water level. In peat, on the other hand, it is frequently advisable to drain below the peat, even if this extends to a depth of six feet or more. If this is impossible owing to lack of sufficient fall, wooden boards should be placed below the drains.

The cheapest method of draining is by a system of mole drainage. I have frequently used a mole drain worked by horses which was made from suggestions by Franks, the Moortown greenkeeper, and myself. It is used as an attachment to the turf-cutting machine. By this method, golf courses on clay land could be drained, previous to the war, at less than a pound per acre.

This mole drain works at the shallow depth of six inches, and is not applicable to agricultural land, as even horses galloping over the ground are sufficient to block the channel. It is, moreover, wonderfully satisfactory on golfing land, especially as supplementary to ordinary tile draining. When the ground is sticky, or any casual water appears, the mole is run through and it becomes absolutely dry at once. This mole drain has a big advantage over the larger one, in that the cut made by the mole is so small that it does not interfere with the lie of the ball.

We have recently used a tractor instead of horses to pull the mole, and have found it a great advantage to do so. The use of the mole provides a solution for the problem of converting the muddiest of clay London courses into good winter links. Experience has proved that the effect lasts for fully ten years.

One of the most remarkable results of its use is that it gets rid of worms. This is probably owing to the fact that it makes the ground so dry that the worms can't work in it.

It also prevents the ground becoming baked during dry summer weather. This is a well-known effect of good drainage, although possibly an unexpected one to the uninitiated. It is largely due to the drainage preventing the ground becoming caked, and also to the encouragement of turf with a good bottom to it.

## TURFING

The cheapest and best method of removing turf is by means of a turf-cutting machine. The thickness of the turf should vary according to the nature of the grasses and the character of the subsoil. As a general rule, turf for greens should be cut as thin as 1½ inches. This is particularly important if the turf contains many tap-rooted weeds; the roots of the weeds, and many of the coarser grasses, are then left behind in the cutting.

In the experience of the writer, it is frequently not a difficult matter to get excellent turf in the immediate neighborhood of a golf course at an extremely cheap rate—a halfpenny a yard or under—and turf obtained from the immediate neighborhood of the course is much more likely to be suitable than turf obtained elsewhere. The writer has known a golf club going to the expense of getting Silloth turf at ninepence a yard, the grasses of which would inevitably disappear and be replaced by those of its environment within a year or two, when much more suitable turf could be obtained from the next field at a cost of a farthing a yard. It should be borne in mind that the most useless turf from a farming point of view is frequently the most valuable for golf. There are many other details which help to lessen the cost of turfing. In an old-established course, turf for new greens, or for renovating old ones, can frequently be obtained from the sides of a neighboring fairway, the sod from which may be replaced by those removed from the site of the green.

There is usually a well-trodden path extending from every tee to the nearest fairway. There is no turf so useful for renovating an old, or making a new tee, as that obtained from a firm path of this kind. The sod removed should be replaced by others, and they in turn get hard and firm.

An important question is the use of manures in turfing. Stable or farmyard manure should almost invariably be placed under the sod: The amount should vary according to the turf and soil. Five loads per green is an average, and on undulating greens the manure should be placed under the raised portions only. The hollows will look after themselves. Manure does more harm than good if dug deeply in: It should be forked in immediately under the sod, and the roots of the finer grasses feed on it at once. If dug in deeply, the coarser grasses are encouraged at the expense of the finer.

On wormy inland courses, considerable expense in worm-killers can frequently be saved by placing a few loads of coke breeze under the sod.

Although the best time to turf is in the late autumn and winter months, sod can, if necessity arises, be laid in certain localities as late as June.

If hot, dry weather arrives, the newly laid sod should be covered with cut grass during the day, and in the evening the grass should be removed so that the dews help to keep the ground moist.

## SEEDING

The writer has known of several instances where ground has been sown, and the result has been so unsatisfactory that after a year or two the land had to be ploughed up and resown.

It is much more economical in the long run to do the thing thoroughly. Mistakes are most frequently made in sowing with the wrong seeds, in not preparing the ground thoroughly beforehand, and in sowing at the wrong time of year.

It is most important that a mixture should be chosen containing a goodly proportion of seeds corresponding to the prevailing grasses of the immediate neighborhood, and seeds should always be obtained from a seed merchant who is not afraid of telling you the exact composition of his mixture. Some seed merchants sell mixtures which are not so valuable for golfing turf as they appear— it is not the best kind of grass which germinates too quickly. Finer turf usually results from a mixture which comes up more slowly but is of a more permanent character. If seeding is necessary, it is frequently advisable to sow with much larger quantity of seed than is customary.

It is of the utmost importance to prepare the land thoroughly before sowing. The ground should be well-drained, the land well-limed when necessary, and fifteen loads to the acre of well-rotted stable manure incorporated with the soil, or a mixture of artificial manure in its stead.

After sowing, see that the birds are scared away by one of the numerous devices suggested for the purpose.

## MANURES

It is surprising how much money can be saved in manures by the help of science, and a sufficient knowledge of chemistry to enable you to judge which are the cheapest and most valuable manures suitable for the soil of the locality with which you have to deal.

It is often advisable to make a point of studying the byproducts of the different industries in the district, as it is obvious that if a suitable manure for the soil can be obtained on the spot, it is obtained cheaper than by rail or cart from a distance. Fish or meat guano, basic slag, malt dust, sulphate of ammonia, chalk, the refuse from leather, cloth, and shoddy factories, seed crushing mills, seaweed, manure extracted from town sewage works, peat moss litter, etc., are all of value under different circumstances.

Basic slag can sometimes be obtained from a neighboring steel works, sulphate of ammonia from a gas works, chalk from a neighboring chalk pit, or seaweed from the seashore. Manures should be used with a considerable amount of discretion and only in small quantities at a time. I have known a considerable amount of damage done by the unintelligent use of artificials. For example, artificials are of the greatest possible value for golfing turf, but they should always be used in small quantities but frequently, and be well diluted with soil or sand and only used during moist weather. A mixture consisting of superphosphate of lime, sulphate of ammonia, and sulphate of potash, supplies most of the feeding material that is necessary for golf, and the experiments at Rothamstead conclusively prove that the character of the grasses can be completely altered by varying the proportion of the different constituents of this mixture.

Sulphate of ammonia is the most valuable of the constituents of this mixture, but I have known of several greens (including even St. Andrews) temporarily ruined by using sulphate of ammonia injudiciously. It should never be put on a green undiluted, as, like most artificials, it has a great affinity for water, and in dry weather absorbs the water from the grasses and burns them up. It also should never be used if the land is the least bit sour, as it simply increases this sourness.

A greenkeeper should attempt to get a sufficient knowledge of botany and chemistry to know, by the character of the herbage of his greens, the kind and the amount of manure that is required. Greenkeepers sometimes think that if they use twice the usual quantity of a manure, it will have double the effect; the exact contrary is the case, as the green may be ruined entirely.

The most important manure of all is cut grass. If the cut grass is always left on the greens and fairways, very little manuring is necessary. On the other hand, if the grass is constantly removed year after year (unless a considerable amount of manure is added to take its place), the turf becomes impoverished and full of weeds. One of the unexpected results of leaving the grass on is that less mowing is necessary. This is probably due to the fact that the growth goes into the roots and not into the leaves.

Mowing without the box on is of special importance on sandy or seaside courses.

## SAND

Sand is often an expensive item on an inland course. It is surprising how frequently a good class of sand is found in pockets on a course or in the immediate neighborhood. A knowledge of geology and botany will enable you to foretell where sand is likely to be found.

On several occasions on visiting a course, I have been told that there was no sand in the district, and have been able to find some by noting the character of the trees, grasses, etc. Sand may be economized by the method in which bunkers are made. It will be noticed in the photographs reproduced that most of the hollows have been turfed, but have been formed in such a way that a ball gravitates towards the sand, which is thrown up against the face. Bunkers of this description have a much more natural appearance, and the amount of sand needed is also considerably less than usual.

## CONSTRUCTING NEW COURSES

## SEASIDE COURSES

*By H.S. Colt:*

The nature of the soil is, no doubt, of great importance, but frequently there is no choice. The rolling sand dunes of the seashore cannot be always ready at hand for our course. It has only three or four times fallen to my lot to help in the construction of a course under these ideal conditions, and very pleasant work it was. There are some common difficulties in dealing with ground of this description. It often lies in a narrow strip by the shore, and the clubhouse is erected at one end of the selected site. In many cases force of circumstances insists upon this, but in others it can be avoided, and if the house be pitched more in the center of the land the wind will be split up between the two nine holes and two starting points will also be provided.

*Wind*—Everyone knows how pleasant it is, after striving against a strong wind and hitting harder and harder at each hole with less and less result, to turn one's back upon the gale for a hole or two and play gigantic shots down wind. After doing this we are refreshed, and feel in a mood to battle with the "brute" who tries to destroy our best efforts.

*Hummocks*—The sandy hummocks common to all of the best of the seaside courses, whilst being one of their finest features, also present some difficulty. On a new course it is often a hard matter to get this ground into good playing order, the covering of turf is so easily broken, especially on a downward slope in dry weather. When these hummocks are covered with good, sound turf they make excellent features and give difficult stances and lies; but at the start of a new course they are liable to be terrible traps. The expense of covering a large tract of this ground with turf must be very considerable, and quite beyond the means of most clubs, and so we often find that the "spirit-level" has been applied and some of the best features of the course flattened out, and a beautiful natural piece of golfing ground reduced to the level of a flat field. With a little patience these hummocks may be made "sound" by light and frequent dressings of rich sandy soil in which suitable seed has been mixed. A dressing composed of heavy soil will almost certainly prove a failure, and the seed mixture should correspond as nearly as possible to the varieties of grasses which exist in the natural turf.

On some sites a certain amount of judicious levelling will be needed, as otherwise the goat of Andrew Kirkaldy's story will be a more suitable inhabitant for the links than the perspiring golfer; but on the margins of the course there can hardly be too many sand dunes. As a guide on this point, the Old Course at St. Andrews seems to me to be a perfect example.

For bunkering work it is impossible to have better materials than these sandy hummocks, as, if the faces are just torn out, we obtain perfectly natural looking hazards, thoroughly in keeping with the surroundings of the links. Yet how often do we see horrible symmetrical-looking pits, with faces smoothed out to the same angle, and the pleasant surroundings spoilt thereby! And very likely some old railway sleepers are used to prevent the sides of the hazards ever looking natural. What can be more incongruous in a sand bunker on a seaside course? They are no doubt useful laid lengthwise on the ground to form a narrow pathway; but, for preventing the sand from blowing, bent grasses, such as Ammophila arundinacea and Elymus arenarius, will do the work efficiently and look natural, and, to keep the sides from falling in, nothing is better than turf laid so as to form a rough, uneven face. But the sides of the bunkers can be allowed to become rugged and irregular in appearance, and not scraped with a spade, as if an asparagus bed were being constructed. The first time that I played over the Prince's Course at Sandwich, one of the many delightful features that appealed to me was that the faces of the bunkers were invariably irregular in appearance, and I believe that these bunkers were, so to speak, "dragged out" with forks or other implements, and spades were not used at all for the work.

*Water*—The water supply is another difficulty common to seaside courses, and this has driven many to select hollows for the putting greens and not plateau. Ground of the latter description is liable to become parched in the summer, when the golfing season is at its height. On many inland links the summer months are generally the slackest; if the greens are not quite perfect then, it does not matter so much as in the spring and autumn. At one time I thought that water was not a necessity, but recent experience has made me alter my opinion, unless the rainfall for the district is well above the average. With an artificial supply of water, many extra opportunities are given to the designer of a golf course. He need not consider whether a certain acceptable site for a putting green is likely to dry up too quickly if it is on a slope facing the south or lies on a plateau. A plentiful supply of water from a reliable source, with a good pressure, so that three or four greens can be watered at the same time, will help largely towards the success of a club, as there can be then very little excuse for bad putting greens. Sometimes artesian wells are sunk at convenient places, and portable oil engines brought into operation to work the pumps. But there is often a risk of the supply of water becoming brackish, and although a slight amount of salt there in will not matter, and may even do some good, if it be present beyond a certain percentage the result will be bad.

*Treatment*—The soil varies greatly on seaside courses, and not only on different courses, but on the same links. On some there is a good depth, and on others the merest sprinkling, and in such cases frequent dressings of light, rich soil must be applied. These, with the help of the horse roller, will improve the turf better than anything else. We must get a firm surface, and when the dressing has worked in to some extent, the roller can be used. It is dangerous to apply a thick dressing of heavy soil, as it may cake on the surface and very likely kill the grass underneath. After the application of a dressing I always like to see the tips of the grass shoots above the soil, and the plants not completely smothered. But when enriching the soil it is quite possible to overdo it, and gradually change the character of the turf to such an extent that we have almost good fatting land for bullocks instead of a clean, close-growing turf suitable for the game of golf. As soon as an even, firm coat of turf is obtained we must stop enriching the soil and watch proceedings. If the course deteriorates, let us at once give it some help, but not until we see some slight sign of this coming about. In the dressing some good Peruvian guano can be added, and from my experience there is no better manure for this purpose; and in the case of all new courses, add some seed to the dressing. There is sure to be a lot of moss and weeds present in the rough covering of the land, and constant slight renovations with seed are certain to give good results. The expense is very small, and I would use it not only in the early autumn and spring dressings, but also through the winter, as if mild weather intervenes the seed will germinate, and the loss of young plants will be but slight. I have recently had quite a success, although the seed was sown late in November; no doubt there was a risk, but we had to renovate the course after an abnormally dry summer, and the saving of time justified the risk.

It will be best to turf the very worst portions of the course, if it is possible to do so, and a little rich soil there under, especially on mounds, will do good; but it is often difficult to get the turf, and then we have to rely on seed.

In constructing a new course it is advisable to make a grass nursery, as a supply of turf is constantly needed for repairs and for new greens and teeing grounds. Four or five acres of good turf generally prove to be one of the club's most valuable assets. Good ground should be selected for the site, and if a little moist (not a swamp) so much the better, as the young plants will develop quicker.

All new courses want careful nursing, and this applies even more to new seaside courses than to others, and constant rolling, dressing, and seeding during the spring, autumn, and winter will work wonders in a comparatively short time. The construction of the teeing grounds and putting greens is dealt with in another chapter.

## HEATHER COURSES

The heathland course has of late years come into special prominence. Walton Heath, Sunningdale, Woking, and Worplesdon are all instances of popular links of this description, and there are many others. As a class they particularly appeal to me, and, although it may seem almost heresy to say so, the best heather courses always appear to me to be quite as good from a golfing point of view as the majority of the seaside links. There are many who can see no merit in anything inland; but, on the other hand, there are many who can see but little merit in some of the much-vaunted seaside courses, and the admirers of the best inland links are an increasing body. We cannot have a St. Andrews or a Hoylake, but we can have something up to the standard of the majority of the seaside courses, although suffering from the disadvantages of being inland.

*Expense*—Construction of a course in a heather country is very costly, as the heather has to be ploughed up in the first place, the roots burnt, probably a large quantity of manure added, and grass seed sown over the whole of the playing area. You cannot get any good result under a year, and it generally means two years at least before the turf is really sound; and if the expense of a full-length course of this description works out at less than four thousand or five thousand pounds, it is cheap, unless there be special advantageous circumstances.

*Drainage*—In many of these courses there is a large amount of peat, and when the turf really begins to take root it seems to stand the drought well, owing to the decayed vegetation in the soil known as humus. But this very advantage may end in disaster unless care be taken to drain the subsoil. One green at Sunningdale had always been a mystery to me; it lay high, had plenty of soil for the roots of the grass, was always carefully nursed in bad weather, and yet never seemed to be entirely satisfactory. I remember a year or two ago purchasing some pigs from a farmer, who described the offspring of a certain sow, which he pointed out to me with pride, as really good "doers." It is a somewhat expressive term, and every greenkeeper will know that certain greens are good "doers" and others just the reverse, and this green was amongst the latter. My friend, Hugh McLean, our greenkeeper at Sunningdale, often had rather a puzzled look on his face when we came to it during our weekly inspection. We would examine the top with great care, and at times even crawl about on our hands and knees, much to the annoyance of the people waiting to play their approach shots. It never seemed to be bad enough to lift, and in the summer it was excellent. We cut a small hole or two in it, to see if the roots of the grass were healthy, and looked in the soil for grubs, and, in fact, took endless trouble. Eventually we hardened our hearts and stripped a big section, to the consternation of the members (Hugh and I are becoming accustomed to that), and on digging underneath we came to a bed of peat. It appears that when the course was constructed this soil was carted from a low-lying sour portion of the land and used for the green, and as it had never been broken up into small pieces and mixed with sharp, gritty materials, it had gradually consolidated and become sour. This was easily remedied, and I trust that the green will adopt a better course of life in future.

It is difficult to over-drain a golf course, and on these peaty courses it is most important to pay careful attention to the drainage. There are generally some boggy bits, which at first look hopeless for golf, and it may be necessary for the framework of the links to use them for play. If these places be carefully drained and some coke breeze be used, I have known them to become quite firm and sound. In drainage of this description it would be well to use six inch pipes for the main drains and three inch for the branch drains, which should be laid 2½ to 3 feet under the soil, and on the top of the pipes a six inch coating of gravel would help matters wonderfully. The expense would be considerable, amounting to a total cost of about one shilling per yard for the six inch mains and ninepence per yard for the three inch, but it would be worth it. In some districts the cost might conceivably be less, as labor is expensive with us and cartage and freight high.

*Lime*—There is another matter which is sometimes overlooked in connection with this class of course: It is the application of lime. Everyone who is a gardener knows how rhododendrons flourish amidst peaty surroundings, and at the same time how they dislike chalk. And greenkeepers know—or, at any rate, they ought to know—the necessity for lime being present in the soil if the turf is to be healthy. Some will remember the covering of the course at Sunningdale with a good dressing of lime soon after it was opened for play. Personally, I shall never forget it. Everyone that I met alluded to it; everybody's boots brought it vividly to my mind. The majority had discussed the merits of lime, or rather its demerits, with learned gardeners (probably of the jobbing type), and the adverse verdict was unanimous. The only friends left to me in the club were the three members of the green committee, and they were indeed staunch ones. However, in time the lime disappeared, and the result proved its efficacy. Where previously there was miserable dyspeptic-looking turf we had a good growth of healthy grass, and life became endurable once again. Now it is possible to obtain ground lime which can be spread by a machine of cunning device, so as to give no cause for grumbling, even to the most unfortunate player amongst your members. It is true the first result of lime is to encourage clover, but it is a recognized fact, I believe, amongst well-known authorities on agricultural chemistry that lime is a necessity for healthy grass, and if there is none in the soil, then it must be applied.

*Porous Surface*—Mention must be made of one more common difficulty with regard to this class of course—the necessity of obtaining and retaining a porous surface for the turf. This sort of soil is very liable to cake on the top, and if this happens it is quite impossible to get a healthy growth. Any sharp, gritty material, free from dangerous chemicals, worked into the surface will keep it porous. Worms will do this, but they are most obnoxious to golfers, and so we have to use artificial means to effect it. Charcoal is very useful, and also keeps the soil sweet; coke breeze, ground clinkers, and sharp sand are all good, and there are, no doubt, many other hard, gritty materials suitable for the purpose.

*General Treatment*—The first thing to do when starting to make a course in a country of this description is to cut down the heather close to the surface, rake it into heaps, and burn it. Then plough the land with the ploughshare set as deeply as possible, and cross-plough the site. Afterwards a subsoil plough can be used, as it is advisable to get as deep a cultivation as possible, and I should not now be satisfied with less than about twelve inches. Harrows can then be put on, and the roots of the heather collected and burnt in slow fires, so that the ashes will be of use presently for the grass. It may be necessary to plough and harrow the land several times so as to get a good fine tilth. As soon as this has been obtained, a dressing of lime, containing a percentage of about ninety-eight percent of carbonate of lime, can be given at the rate of about one ton to the acre; after this is well slaked and all the burning properties consumed, the manure can be spread on the surface. Rich horse manure, short and free from straw, should be obtained and used at the rate of from fifteen to twenty tons to the acre—less in the case of good land, and even more in the case of very poor land. Let this be harrowed into the soil, and then the surface can be rolled either with a Cambridge roller or an ordinary double-cylinder roller, a dry day being chosen for the work.

It is better to let the land consolidate as much as possible before sowing the seed, and if the seedbed is prepared in this way a month or six weeks before sowing, so much the better. After ploughing has been finished and a fine tilth obtained, it is almost impossible to have the land too firm, as the seed will grow much better in a solid bed than in loose soil. I have always noticed that the seed germinates better in the tracks of the wheels of a cart, which has passed over the land after sowing has taken place, than in the adjoining ground; one can see the marks of the wheels quite plainly by a dense growth of grass.

If there is plenty of time (there generally is a rush to get the work done) it will give an opportunity to rid the site of weeds, which have grown in the meantime, before the seed is sown. A still day should be selected for sowing, and a very useful machine is sold for this operation at quite a moderate price, called the Little Wonder Sowing Machine. An even distribution of seed can be depended upon by using it and by employing an intelligent man, who walks at an even pace up and down the quarter to be sown, pegs being used at the ends of the portion dealt with. It is better to sow twice than only once, using about two-thirds of the allotted amount in the first sowing, and then the remaining one-third across the land. If eight bushels to the acre be used, a thick turf should be obtained quickly; and it is better, in my opinion, to use, as a general rule, the finest mixture of seeds, and pay more for it, than to purchase a cheaper mixture with rye grass. The comparative increase in the total cost of the construction of the course is but slight. Rye grass germinates more quickly than the finer grasses, and in some places, like the Riviera, this is of enormous importance, and it is advisable to use it under such circumstances; but I would prefer not to do so in England unless compelled by other reasons. The early autumn—say, the first week in September—is an excellent time to sow, and I have had better results by choosing that time than in any other period. For experimental purposes I have sown seed during almost every month of the year and, sowing to exceptional weather, had some very amusing results. Another favorite time to sow is early in March. For the North of England it is better to be later in the spring than in the South. After the seed is sown the ground should be very carefully hand-raked, and the men should be watched so that they do not leave little furrows in the land from the prongs of the rakes; otherwise the grass will come up in long lines and not indiscriminately on the surface, which is what we want to see. When this has been done, the surface can be heavily rolled on a dry day; the roller is generally used far too little for this process of cultivation, and, at the risk of repetition, let us remember that the firmer the seedbed the better the germination is sure to be.

Having now worked hard and taken every precaution, we shall surely be entitled to a little relaxation, and see the young plants come up and grow and flourish, and a beautiful fine sward appear in next to no time. And so we shall if we have luck; but all sorts of calamities are likely to happen. Terrific rain will possibly come upon us and wash the seed from the hills to the hollows; a very severe frost may seize upon the young plants and check them badly, if not kill them; and a long spell of dry east wind may wither them, and a summer of tropical heat and record droughts may step in upon us and destroy the young turf which, to our great joy, was growing so well. In fact, the plagues of Egypt seem but slight evils in comparison with the trials sometimes experienced by the keen and anxious greenkeeper. We have all passed through bad times in connection with new courses, and the general golfing public have never yet realized that sometimes it is not an exceedingly easy matter to turn a large area of land into perfect golfing turf in a few short months. Only constant supervision and careful nursing can bring this about, and sometimes even then the fates are against us, and we have to put up with ridiculous criticism from the owner of a small villa, who has perhaps, after many years of close attention, got a little patch of indifferent grass to grow in a sort of way in his back garden. When eventually we do succeed, the result compensates us for any small irritation we may have suffered, possibly none too meekly, in the past, as, given a nice, fine, bright day in the early spring or autumn, a course like Sunningdale and others of the same description appeals to the weary man as few other things do. The green turf, with its background of heather, has a fascination to the eye which it is difficult to excel; and if the course has been "carved out," to use Mr. Croome's words, in an irregular, rugged manner, and the artificial work properly concealed, the effect is indeed pleasing. Golfers are, moreover, becoming now more and more sensitive to the artistic side of golf courses, and the man who just ploughs round in an entirely golfing spirit is getting rarer every day. I know it well from the outcry which is raised if a hole is changed and an intruding Scotch fir tree has to be sacrificed. The old custom of squaring off the course and greens in rectangular fashion is departing, and instead we find an irregular course, with a bay of turf here and there and a promontory of heather to slightly turn the line of play to right or left as the case may be, and the result is desirable in every way. And if the heather be never levelled off, but allowed to encroach a little even on the margins, it will appear as if it were naturally growing into the turf, and the artificiality be further reduced. Everyone knows how pretty a border of flowers looks when the plants are allowed to grow over the edge and on to the paths, and the gardener's trimming instincts are checked with a firm hand. The same thing applies to heather golf courses. The margins of heather prove excellent hazards, and the sod used for the banks of bunkers are all in keeping with the character of the district. We can also employ such sod to make walls for our shelters, which, if thatched with the local plant, will enable us to avoid the erection of little suburban tea houses which so often find their way into unsuitable surroundings. Heather mounds and pots form also useful hazards, and a pleasant change from wet, congealed sand, which is so often the alternative.

There is only one more point which I desire to bring forward in connection with heather courses. A thick layer of impervious ironstone often exists under the surface, and some consider that it is essential to break through this crust, commonly called "the pan," before attempting to grow turf. I have found that if drains are laid on the top of it to carry off the surplus water, very good results can be obtained, and as it is often two feet or more below the surface, an enormous expense is avoided.

## COMMONS

Now let us consider a totally different proposition, and not nearly such a difficult one so far as the cultural part is concerned—the case of constructing a golf course on a common. If we have a large tract of good old turf growing on a light, sandy soil with gravel underneath, without the semblance of a hedge, with clumps of whin bushes, broom, and bracken, and some pleasant undulations, and one or two bold features thrown in, there is not much room for complaint, and there is a prospect of some very enjoyable golf. However, two difficulties exist—the commoners and the commonable beasts. The commoners need at times a lot of tact—the commonable beasts an even temper and considerable patience. Both are apt to resent interference with their rights; the former retaliate at times by digging up the best putting green with their spades, and the latter by destroying it with their hoofs. The best plan to get over both difficulties is to encourage the commoners to play golf themselves, and if a club be started for them, and the ways and means provided for them to enjoy the game, the manners of the commonable beasts are apt also to improve. In time an annual match can be held between the parent club and the commoners' club, and during the subsequent convivial evening leave may be obtained for making a few more necessary bunkers, even at the expense of the commonable beast. These hazards must, however, be made with discretion; otherwise a cow or a goat will be sure to fall a victim to them, and break its leg or do some other quite unnecessary and foolish thing.

Then, again, pedestrians have a nasty way of objecting to being hit by a golf ball. I was called in some time ago to advise a club which had a large common at its disposal. I planned what I was pleased to think quite a good course, and left the place in the best of spirits. However, the course was never made. There was one delightful hole, which adjoined some seats used by the public to observe, from a sitting posture, the setting sun. It had certainly been suggested to me, and swept aside as ridiculous, that possibly some of these observers might receive a cruel blow in the back of the neck from a pulled tee shot. And in the end these seats spoilt the course, and, in addition, a beautiful hole with a ravine running parallel to catch a pulled shot, unless stopped by—a seat.

## PARKS

Next, probably, in order of merit comes the park course. But the park must be large, and the soil light, to enable one to lay out a good course. There is of necessity a feeling of restriction when playing the game with a six foot oak paling on every side, and a few roe deer grazing on the horizon do not take this away. The sense of freedom is usually one of the great charms of the game, and it is almost impossible to lay out a big, bold course in a park unless it be of large dimensions, and one needs some three or four hundred acres within the ring fence to prevent the cramped feeling. No doubt many links have been made in parks of from 100 to 150 acres; but is the same pleasure derived from a game under such conditions, as from one played on a course carved out from a large heathery moor or big open common?

The boundary and the trees will probably be the most prominent difficulties in making a course of this description. The first can be got over if there is plenty of land, and it is possible to be extravagant with it and leave a margin so as to avoid constantly seeing the fence. And one can even lay out a course, if the materials be sufficient, to which the well-known term of contempt used by the superior seaside golfer, "It is just park golf," cannot be fairly applied.

*Trees*—The trees are, however, always a difficulty. It is hard to condemn a fine old specimen oak or beech because it comes into the line of play. At Stoke Poges, one fine old beech tree caused me much unpleasantness. It was, unfortunately, right in the line of play of what has, perhaps, turned out to be a satisfactory short hole, with a certain amount of character about it. We tried our best to save the tree, but in the end there was no way out of the difficulty, and it had to go. It is a more or less accepted fact that trees are not the best of hazards, for the obvious reason that they unfortunately afford but slight opportunity for the display of golfing skill in extricating the ball from their clutches. Moreover, during the fall of the leaf they are always a nuisance, and it is exceedingly difficult to grow satisfactory turf under their shade; but they are undoubtedly charming features in a landscape view.

*General Treatment*—On the other hand, there are usually many desirable characteristics in this class of course. The turf, if well rolled down and cut close, works up very quickly, and if the soil be light, it almost becomes too good for the game; but old turf of this description will stand a vast amount of heavy rolling between the greens, and a motor-roller is very useful for the work. There are generally many pleasant looking undulations and ravines, and almost invariably some water hazards, although, with the present heavy balls and their equally heavy price, the latter are not always acceptable to the bad player, nor to the good one, as far as that goes. Abundance of land, light soil, old turf, good drainage, and a few bold features should give an opportunity of making a good course. If there be lakes of many acres in extent, there will be some difficulty in knowing how to deal with them, as it is not much use to ask the long handicap player to lose two and sixpence balls every day of his life. But very often it is possible so to place the hole that the timorous can skirt round the margin, and the player full of natural or artificial courage can "go" for the long carry. Thus the big feature will not be lost to the golf course, and the path of safety provides an answer to the complaint from the loser of new golf balls.

## CLAY COURSES

Now, with many variations, we gradually descend to the last resort of the keen golfer—heavy clay. I have just returned from bunkering such a course. After rising at 5:45 a.m., and missing my train in London owing to the railway line being blocked somewhere below Sunningdale, I arrived an hour and a half late on the scene of operations. A blizzard was blowing from the east, snow was driving into our faces, and the state of the ground was— well, it was wet. A committee of enthusiasts followed me round, and I put in pegs mercilessly, until at last we came to a flat piece of ground about 120 yards long, where a short hole had previously been determined upon. I had not the honor of laying out the course. I let loose the imprisoned venom which was in me, and after bunkering the hole in every possible direction we went in to lunch, and I particularly remember how warm and soothing was a bottle of Pommard, which my kind hosts provided. But I have seen many worse courses than the one in question, and can quite understand the feelings of a visitor to a strange club who, on being asked what he thought of the links, replied that they might have been much worse; and on being further questioned as to what he meant, answered: "Well, you see, there might have been eighteen holes instead of only nine!"

After spending several hours of a raw winter's day in wearily plodding over flat fields with high bullfinch hedges, with one's boots wet through and twice their normal size from gradual accumulations of clay, one is inclined to lose heart and to stop the proposed attempt to play the game within a radius of at least twenty miles from the spot. Some would, no doubt, do this, and at the same time deprive innumerable golfers of ever playing, except during a brief summer holiday. With a clean sweep of the hedges, careful drainage, and good bunkering, an extraordinary change can be effected, especially if whin bushes or clumps of broom can be grown here and there to relieve the monotony, and to break up the flatness; so much so that even a fastidious seaside player may enjoy a game there on a nice warm day in the spring, when the putting greens have become fast and firm owing to the care of a good greenkeeper, and the course has been worked up by rolling and mowing.

But everything depends upon the actual constructive work of such a course. If this has been carried out well and the bunkering made to look as natural as possible, and bath-like pits avoided and nice rugged mounds made, and not a series of pepper-pots or ant-heaps, it is quite possible to play several most enjoyable rounds over such a course during many months of the year, but not during a blizzard from the east in the month of January. What has already been said about drainage and obtaining a porous, firm surface applies especially to clay courses. Cinders can also be used under the turf on the greens; it is, no doubt, as old as the hills, but has hardly been done sufficiently in the construction of golf courses.

# FOREST COURSES

A few years ago no one would have thought of constructing a golf course in a forest, and probably the New Zealand Club's links at Byfleet was the first example. But since then there have been several successful instances both at home and abroad, and some notes about the clearing of the site may be useful.

It is essential to make the clearing bold and wide, as it is not very enjoyable to play down long alleys with trees on either side, and better effects can be obtained from a landscape point of view if this be done. It will be necessary to grub up most of the roots through the course, but a few sparsely scattered ones can be turned into mounds and expense saved, as grubbing is very costly. At the Swinley Forest golf course, we cut down about fourteen thousand, and of these some five thousand were grubbed. I think almost every known method was tried, and with small trees we had a great success with a powerful steam engine. A long wire hawser was attached to the tree at about ten feet from the ground, and the engine gave a grunt and the tree was out of the ground, roots and all. But when this engine tackled a big Scotch fir, a regular battle would ensue; the engine's grunts became loud snorts, and although the betting was at least 100 to 1 on the engine, the tree would make a fine show of resistance. When it gave way all the roots were by no means out of the ground, but only those on the far side to the engine, as when the tree fell the large side branches would get fixed in the earth, and act as effectual brakes to all the efforts of the engine. These roots had afterwards to be grubbed, and meant a large extra expense. The cost of pulling down by the engine, including hire, coal, labor, etc., came to about one shilling per tree;

but the subsequent cost of grubbing the roots of the big trees and getting them out of their holes was enormous in comparison—in fact, so big that I prefer not to mention it. We tried everything—patent root extractors, blasting, haulage by horses, scientific levers, and goodness only knows what else—but had to return always to the British workman with his mattock. The trees by the side of the course need not be grubbed, but can be cut practically level with the surface of the ground by means of cross-cut saws. The stumps can then be bored by drills of about two inches in diameter; saltpetre is then placed in the holes and they are filled up with a little water and corked. After two or three months or so, the corks can be removed and the holes filled with paraffin and then set on fire; by this means the stumps will gradually smolder away. I am indebted for this information to my friend Mr. Hudson, of *Country Life*.

# CHAPTER 12

## Overseeing Construction

*"The work can never be done properly except under occasional expert supervision. Work done without expert supervision is invariably bad." – Alister MacKenzie*

*By Alister MacKenzie:*

Economy in course construction consists in obtaining the best possible results at a minimum of cost. The more one sees of golf courses, the more one realizes the importance of doing construction work really well, so that it is likely to be of a permanent character. It is impossible to lay too much stress on the importance of finality.

Every golfer knows examples of courses which have been constructed and rearranged over and over again, and the fact that all over the country thousands of pounds are flittered away in doing bad work, which will ultimately have to be scrapped, is particularly distressful to a true economist. As an example of unnecessary labor and expense, the writer has in mind a green which has been entirely re-laid on four different occasions. In the first instance, it was of the ridge and furrow type; the turf was then lifted and it was made dead flat. A new secretary was appointed, and he made it a more pronounced ridge and furrow than ever; it was then re-laid and made flat again, and has now been entirely reconstructed with undulations of a more natural outline and appearance.

Perhaps the most serious mistake made by a golf committee is the fallacy that they will save money by neglecting to obtain expert advice in regard to fresh construction work.

Except where the course has been designed and the construction work supervised by the modern golf architect, there is hardly a golf club of any size which has not frittered away hundreds of pounds in doing bad work, all for the want of the best advice in the first instance.

There can be little doubt that the poorer the club, the more important it is for it not to waste its small funds in doing the wrong kind of work, but to get the best possible advice from its inception.

———————•———————

It cannot be too frequently emphasized that in starting a new course or reconstructing an old one, it is of the utmost importance that the committee should have a scheme before them of a definite and final nature. It would be sound finance for the majority of golf clubs to pay the expenses of the green committee for the purpose of visiting good examples of construction work on other courses.

They should not, of necessity, visit courses where leading open competitions are held, as many of the very best clubs rarely offer their courses for competitions.

They should be guided in their choice of architect by a course constructed out of indifferent material, and not by one constructed out of magnificent natural golfing land.

They should take into consideration the cost, the popularity with all classes of players, and the finality and permanency of the work.

Having decided on the architect and having passed the plan, it is as well to take steps to ensure that the construction work is done according to the ideas of the designer.

Experience of advising a hundred golf clubs has convinced the writer that the work can never be done properly except under occasional expert supervision. Work done without expert supervision is invariably bad.

The designer should not be tied down too closely to his original plan. Mature consideration and unexpected changes in the subsoil, etc., may make a modification in the plan necessary to save expense and get better results.

———————

The writer has just returned from a most delightful sand dune country which he chose for his holiday in great pail owing to the fact that he had seen it before and had also seen Mr. Colt's plan for the constructing of what should have been the finest eighteen hole course in England.

On arrival he found the secretary of the committee had, through motives of false economy, refrained from getting Mr. Colt to supervise the work, and had done it themselves. The outcome was an expenditure of three or four times as much money as Mr. Colt would have needed, the destruction of many of the beautiful natural undulations and features which were the making of Mr. Colt's scheme, the conversion of magnificent visible greens into semi-blind ones, banked up like croquet lawns, and a complete absence of turf owing to wrong treatment, and alterations in the placing of the tees, bunkers, and greens, and a total disregard of the beginner and the long-handicap player. On a seaside course in particular, little construction work is necessary; the important thing is to make the fullest possible use of existing features. Five hundred pounds in labor expended under expert supervision is better than ten thousand pounds injudiciously expended.

Surely in the case of a golf club it is more important to have an architect for the course, and any new work on the course, than for the clubhouse. Much greater mistakes are made in constructing the former than in building the latter.

---

The architect is the best judge in deciding how often he should visit a course for supervision purposes. How often have I heard from the secretary, who is almost invariably a cheery optimist, that the construction work was going on splendidly, and when too late discovered that hundreds of pounds had been thrown away in doing bad work which had ultimately to be scrapped! There is an old Persian saying:

"He who knows not, and knows not that he knows not, is a fool. Avoid him."

"He who knows not, and knows that he knows not, will learn. Teach him."

"He who knows, and knows not that he knows, will fail. Pity him."

"He who knows, and knows that he knows, is a wise man. Follow him."

# APPENDIX A

## Selected Courses by Alister MacKenzie

- Alwoodley Golf Club, Leeds, England
- Augusta National Golf Club, Augusta, Georgia, USA
- Bingley St Ives Golf Course, Harden, Bingley, West Yorkshire, England
- Blackpool Park Golf Club, Lancashire, England
- Burning Tree Club, Bethesda, Maryland, USA
- Cavendish Golf Club, Buxton, Derbyshire, England
- Claremont Country Club, Oakland, California, USA
- Cork Golf Club, Cork, Ireland
- Crowborough Beacon Golf Club, East Sussex, England
- Crystal Downs Country Club, Frankfort, Michigan, USA
- Cypress Point Club, Monterey Peninsula, California, USA
- Duff House Royal Golf Club, Aberdeenshire, Scotland
- Garforth Golf Club, Leeds, England
- Green Hills Country Club, Millbrae, California, USA
- Haggin Oaks Golf Course, Sacramento, California, USA
- Hazel Grove Golf Club, Cheshire, England

- The No. 1 course at Hazlehead Park, Aberdeen, Scotland
- Jockey Club, Buenos Aires, Argentina
- Knock Golf Club, County Antrim, Northern Ireland
- The Old Course at Lahinch Golf Club, County Clare, Ireland
- Meadow Club, Fairfax, California, USA
- Moortown Golf Club, Leeds, England
- Nenagh Golf Club, Co Tipperary, Ireland
- Northwood Golf Club, Monte Rio, California, USA
- Pasatiempo Golf Club, Santa Cruz, California, USA
- Pitreavie (Dunfermline) Golf Club, Fife, Scotland
- The Portland Course at the Royal Troon Golf Club, Troon, Scotland
- Reddish Vale Golf Course, Stockport, England
- Redlands Country Club, Redlands, California, USA
- Rosemont Course at Blairgowie Golf Club, Perth and Kinross, Scotland
- Royal Adelaide Golf Club, Adelaide, Australia
- Seaton Carew Golf Club Course, Seaton Carew, Durham County, England
- The Scarlet Course at The Ohio State University, Columbus, Ohio, USA
- St. Charles Country Club, Winnipeg, Manitoba, Canada
- Sharp Park Golf Course, Pacifica, California, USA
- Sitwell Park Golf Club, Rotherham, England
- Teignmouth Golf Club, Devon, England
- Titirangi Golf Club, Titirangi, Auckland, New Zealand
- University of Michigan Golf Course, University of Michigan, Ann Arbor, Michigan, USA

- The Valley Club of Montecito Santa Barbara, California, USA
- West Course at Royal Melbourne Golf Club, Melbourne, Australia
- Willingdon Golf Club, East Sussex, England
- Worcester Golf & Country Club, Worcestershire, England

# APPENDIX B

## Selected Courses by H.S. Colt

- Belvoir Park Golf Club, Belfast, Northern Ireland
- Clyne Common, Gower Peninsula, Wales
- Country Club of Detroit, Detroit, Michigan, USA
- Fresh Meadow Country Club, Lake Success, New York, USA
- Ganton Golf Club, Ganton, North Yorkshire, England
- Golf de Granville Baie du Mont St Michel, Granville, Normandy, France
- Hamilton Golf and Country Club, Ancaster, Ontario, Canada
- Milwaukee Golf Course, River Hills, Wisconsin, USA
- Moor Park Golf Club, Rickmansworth, Hertfordshire, England
- North Shore Country Club, Glenview, Illinois, USA
- The Park Country Club, Williamsville, New York, USA
- Royal County Down Golf Club, Newcastle, County Down, Northern Ireland
- The Royal Dublin Golf Club, Bull Island, Dublin, Ireland
- Royal Liverpool Golf Club, Merseyside, England

- Royal Lytham & St Annes Golf Club, Lancashire, England
- Royal Portrush Golf Club, County Antrim, Northern Ireland
- St Georges Hill Golf Club, Weybridge, Surrey, England
- Toronto Golf Club, Mississauga, Ontario, Canada
- Wentworth Club, Virginia Water, Surrey, England

# APPENDIX C

## Selected Courses by A.W. Tillinghast

- Alpine Country Club, Alpine, New Jersey, USA
- Anglo-American Club, Lac L'Achigan, Quebec, Canada
- Bailey Park Country Club, Mt. Vernon, New York, USA
- Baltimore Country Club, Baltimore, Maryland, USA
- Baltusrol Golf Club, Springfield, New Jersey, USA
- Belmont Park Golf Club, Richmond, Virginia, USA
- Berkshire Hills Country Club, Pittsfield, Massachusetts, USA
- Bethpage State Park, Farmingdale, New York, USA
- Binghamton Country Club, Endwell, New York, USA
- Bluff Point Golf Club, Plattsburg, New York, USA
- Brackenridge Park Golf Club, San Antonio, Texas, USA
- Brook Hollow Golf Club, Dallas, Texas, USA
- Cedarbrook Hill Country Club, Philadelphia, Pennsylvania, USA
- Davis Shores Country Club, St. Augustine, Florida, USA
- Elmwood Country Club, White Plains, New York, USA
- Erie Golf Club, Pennsylvania, USA

- Essex County Country Club, West Orange, New Jersey, USA
- Fenway Golf Club, Scarsdale, New York, USA
- Forest Hill Field Club, Bloomfield, New Jersey, USA
- Fort Sam Houston Golf Club, La Oma Course, Fort Sam Houston, Texas, USA
- Golden Valley Country Club, Golden Valley, Minnesota, USA
- Indian Hills Country Club, Mission Hills, Kansas, USA
- Irem Temple Country Club, Dallas, Pennsylvania, USA
- Island Hills Golf Club, Sayville, New York, USA
- Johnson City Country Club, Johnson City, Tennessee, USA
- Jumping Brook Country Club, Neptune, New Jersey, USA
- Kansas City Country Club, Mission Hills, Kansas, USA
- Knollwood Country Club, Elmsford, New York, USA
- Lafayette Country Club, Jamesville, New York, USA
- Lakewood Country Club, Westlake, Ohio, USA
- Marble Island Golf Club, Colchester, Vermont, USA
- Mount Pleasant Country Club, Browns Mills, New Jersey, USA
- New Castle Country Club, New Castle, Pennsylvania, USA
- Newport Country Club, Newport, Rhode Island, USA
- Norfolk Country Club, Norfolk, Connecticut, USA
- North Shore Country Club, Glen Head, New York, USA
- Oak Hills Country Club, San Antonio, Texas, USA
- Oaks Country Club, Tulsa, Oklahoma, USA
- Old Oaks Country Club, Purchase, New York, USA

- Paramount Country Club, New City, New York, USA
- Philadelphia Cricket Club, Philadelphia, Pennsylvania, USA
- Quaker Ridge Golf Club, Scarsdale, New York, USA
- Rainey Estate Golf Club, Lilliput, Huntington, New York, USA
- Ridgewood Country Club, Paramus, New Jersey, USA
- Rochester Golf & Country Club, Rochester, Minnesota, USA
- Rockaway Hunting Club, Cedarhurst, New York, USA
- San Francisco Golf Club, San Francisco, California, USA
- Sands Point Golf Club, Sands Point, New York, USA
- Saxon Woods Golf Club, Scarsdale, New York, USA
- Scarsdale Golf Club, Hartsdale, New York, USA
- Shackamaxon Country Club, Scotch Plains, New Jersey, USA
- Shawnee Country Club, East Stroudsburg, Pennsylvania, USA
- Somerset Hills Country Club, Bernardsville, New Jersey, USA
- Southward Ho Country Club, Bay Shore, New York, USA
- Suburban Golf Club, Union, New Jersey, USA
- Suneagles Golf Club at Fort Monmouth, Eatontown, New Jersey, USA
- Sunnehanna Country Club, Johnstown, Pennsylvania, USA
- Swope Memorial Golf Club, Kansas City, Missouri, USA
- Tulsa Country Club, Tulsa, Oklahoma, USA
- Upper Montclair Country Club, Clifton, New Jersey,

USA

- Winged Foot Golf Club, Mamaroneck, New York, USA
- Wyoming Valley Country Club, Wilkes-Barre, Pennsylvania, USA

# ABOUT THE PUBLISHER

Coventry House Publishing is a traditional publisher of adult fiction and non-fiction titles. Founded in Dublin, Ohio in 2012, we're beginning a long tradition of serving readers and authors across the country, one book at a time.

We pride ourselves on the quality, meaningful work we publish. Our primary genres of focus include business & economics, sports & recreation, education & social science, and fiction & entertainment. Please visit our website, www.coventrybooks.com, for more information about our featured books and authors.

# INDEX

CPSIA information can be obtained at www.ICGtesting.com
Printed in the USA
LVOW07s0958020815

448532LV00013B/449/P